what's cooking
thai

Christine France

p

This is a Parragon Publishing book
First published in 2004

Parragon Publishing
Queen Street House
4 Queen Street
Bath BA1 1HE
United Kingdom

ISBN: 1-40542-541-5

Printed in China

ACKNOWLEDGEMENTS
PHOTOGRAPHY: Colin Bowling, Paul Forrester, and Stephen Brayne

NOTE

This book uses imperial, metric, or US cup measurements. Follow the same units of measurement throughout;
do not mix imperial and metric. All spoon measurements are level: teaspoons are assumed to be 5 ml
and tablespoons are assumed to be 15 ml. Unless otherwise stated, milk is assumed to be whole, eggs and
individual vegetables such as potatoes are medium, and pepper is freshly ground black pepper.

The times given for each recipe are an approximate guide only. The preparation times may differ according to
the techniques used by different people and the cooking times may vary as a result of the type of oven used.
Ovens should be preheated to the specified temperature. If using a fan-assisted oven, check the manufacturer's
instructions for adjusting the time and temperature. The preparation times include chilling
and marinating times, where appropriate.

Recipes using raw or very lightly cooked eggs should be avoided by infants, the elderly,
pregnant women, convalescents, and anyone suffering from an illness.

contents

introduction

Anyone who has a love of Thai food will appreciate that it is a unique cuisine, distinctly different from the countries which border it geographically, but with many clear foreign influences. Many of its characteristics are due to climate and culture, but a history of many centuries of invasions and emigration has played a large part in shaping Thai cuisine.

The roots of the Thai nation can be traced back to the first century, in the time of the Chinese Han Dynasty, when the T'ai tribes occupied parts of South China, along valuable trade routes between the East and West. Over the years, the T'ai had a close but often stormy relationship with the Chinese, and eventually began to emigrate south to the lands of what is now North Thailand, bordering Burma and Cambodia, then sparsely occupied by Buddhist and Hindu tribes.

Eventually, the T'ai established the independent Kingdom of Sukhothai (translated as "dawn of happiness"), eventually known as Siam. The ports of Siam formed the entry to an important trade route, where ships from all over Europe and Japan docked in the coastal ports or sailed up the rivers bringing foreign foods, teas and spices, silks, copper, and ceramics. It was the Portuguese who, in the sixteenth century, introduced the chile to this part of the world, where the plants thrived and continue to thrive. Trade with Arab and Indian merchants was important, too, and many Muslims settled in Siam. The Kingdom of Siam survived until the twentieth century, when in 1939 it became the constitutional monarchy of Thailand.

Present day Thailand still reflects much of these centuries of mixed cultures, and the Thai people are independent, proud, creative, and passionate. Their love of life is clear in the way they take pleasure in eating and entertaining. They love to eat, at any time of day, and the streets are lined with food vendors selling a huge variety of tasty snacks from their stalls, carts, or bicycles all day long.

Thai people love parties and celebrations, and during their many festivals, the colorful, often elaborate and carefully prepared festive foods show a respect for custom and tradition. Visitors are entertained with endless trays of tasty snacks, platters of exotic fruits, and Thai beer or local whiskey. When a meal is served, all the dishes are served up together, so the cook can enjoy the food along with the guests. Thais take pride in presenting food beautifully, often carving vegetables into elaborate shapes as garnishes. Their intricate and skilled artistry is an important part of Thai culture, and shows a deep appreciation of beautiful things.

Everyday life in Thailand is closely tied to the seasons, marked by the harvesting of crops and vagaries of the monsoon climate. The Thai people take their food seriously, taking great care in choosing the freshest ingredients and carefully balancing delicate flavors and textures. Throughout Thailand, rice is the most important staple food, the center of every meal, and coconut in its various forms has an almost equal place. Cooks in every region are expert at making the most of the food that's locally available, so the character of many dishes will vary depending on the region.

FUNDAMENTALS OF THAI CUISINE

Essential ingredients when you're starting out to cook your own Thai cuisine are coconut, lime, chile, rice, garlic, lemon grass, ginger, and cilantro, and with a basic supply of these you can create many Thai dishes. Although many recipes have long lists of ingredients, the methods are simple enough for even an inexperienced cook to handle.

The main principle of Thai cooking is balance, the five extremes of bitter, sour, hot, salt, and sweet being carefully and skillfully balanced within a dish, or over several courses, each dish contributing part of the whole perfect balance of the entire meal.

BASIL
Three types of sweet basil are used in Thai cooking, and the sweet basil we can buy in the West works well. Asian grocery stores often sell the seeds for Thai basil, so you can grow your own.

CHILES
The many varieties of chile vary in heat, from very mild to fiery hot, so choose carefully. The small red or green Thai chiles often used in Thai dishes are very hot, so if you prefer a mild heat, remove the seeds. Red are generally slightly sweeter and milder than green. Larger chiles tend to be milder. Dried crushed chiles are used for seasoning.

CILANTRO
This is a fresh herb with a pungent, citruslike flavor, widely used in savory dishes. Try to buy it with the root still attached.

COCONUT MILK
This is made from grated and pressed fresh coconut. It can be bought in cans, in powdered form or in blocks (creamed coconut). Coconut cream is skimmed from the top, and is slightly thicker and richer.

GALANGAL
A relative of ginger with a milder, aromatic flavor. Available fresh or dried.

GARLIC
Used whole, crushed, sliced, or chopped in savory dishes and curry pastes. Pickled garlic is another useful item and makes an attractive garnish.

GINGER
Fresh ginger is peeled and grated, chopped or sliced for a warm spicy flavor.

JAGGERY
This is a rich, brown unrefined sugar from the coconut palm, sold in solid blocks, and the best way to use it is to crush with a mallet or rolling pin. Dark brown sugar is an acceptable substitute.

KAFFIR LIME LEAVES
The leaves have a distinctive lime scent, and can be bought fresh, dried or frozen.

LEMON GRASS
An aromatic tropical grass with a lemony scent similar to lemon balm. Strip off the fibrous outer leaves and slice or finely chop the rest or bruise and use whole.

RICE VINEGAR
This is used as a savory flavoring. White wine vinegar can be substituted if it is unavailable.

RICE WINE
This is made from fermented glutinous rice or millet. Dry sherry makes an acceptable substitute.

SOY SAUCE
Both dark and light soy sauces are used for seasoning, but light is saltier than dark. Use light soy sauce for stir-fries, or with light meats. Dark soy sauce adds a rich flavor and color to braised red meat dishes.

TAMARIND PASTE
The pulp of the tamarind fruit is usually sold in blocks and has a sour/sweet flavor. Soak in hot water for 30 minutes, press out the juice, and discard the rest.

THAI FISH SAUCE
Called *nam pla*, this is used like salt for seasoning. It is made from salted, fermented fish.

appetizers, snacks & soups

The structure of a Thai meal is more flexible than in the West, with no appetizers and main courses as such. Instead, soups, side dishes, noodles, rice, and main dishes appear simultaneously. Snacks or appetizers may be served in the afternoon or offered to guests before a meal.

Many of the recipes in this section are savory snacks that are eaten at all times of day and at parties and celebrations. The Thais eat when they are hungry, and street vendors cater for this need with a huge and tempting array of wares from their stalls and bicycles—each street vendor has his own speciality of fast food, from crab cakes to spareribs, and steamed mussels to rice soup.

Soups are part of almost every Thai meal, including breakfast. Lunch is often a bowl of hearty soup—a thin stock-based broth, usually spiked with red or green chiles, and with the addition of fine noodles, rice, egg strips, or tiny fish balls, meatballs, or cubes of tofu. In restaurants, soups are often served in a large "firepot" with a central funnel of burning coals to keep the contents hot.

jumbo shrimp rolls

with sweet soy sauce

serves 4

15 minutes

10 minutes

dip
1 small fresh red Thai chile, seeded
1 tsp honey
4 tbsp soy sauce

rolls
2 tbsp fresh cilantro leaves
1 garlic clove
1 1/2 tsp Thai red curry paste
16 won ton skins
1 egg white, lightly beaten
16 raw jumbo shrimp, shelled and tails left intact
corn oil, for deep-frying

These crisp, golden-fried little mouthfuls are packed with flavor and served with a hot and sweet soy dip—perfect to stimulate appetites at the start of a meal, or as a tasty hot snack.

variation

If you prefer, replace the won ton wrappers with phyllo pastry—use a long strip of pastry, place the paste and a shrimp on one end, then brush with egg white and wrap the pastry round the shrimp to enclose and deep-fry.

To make the dip, finely chop the chile and place in a small bowl. Add the honey and soy and stir well. Set aside until required.

To make the shrimp rolls, finely chop the cilantro and garlic and place in a bowl. Add the curry paste and mix well.

Brush each won ton skin with egg white and place a small dab of the cilantro mixture in the center. Place a shrimp on top.

Fold the won ton skin over, enclosing the shrimp and leaving the tail exposed. Repeat with the other shrimp.

Heat the oil for deep-frying in a large, heavy-bottom pan to 350°–375°F/180°–190°C, or until a cube of bread browns in 30 seconds. Deep-fry the shrimp in small batches for 1–2 minutes each, until golden brown and crisp. Drain on paper towels and serve with the dip.

shrimp & chicken
sesame toasts

makes 72 pieces

15 minutes

15 minutes

4 skinless, boneless chicken thighs
3 1/2 oz/100 g cooked shelled shrimp
1 small egg, beaten
3 scallions, finely chopped
2 garlic cloves, crushed
2 tbsp chopped fresh cilantro
1 tbsp Thai fish sauce
1/2 tsp pepper

1/4 tsp salt
12 slices white bread, crusts removed
generous 1/3 cup sesame seeds
corn oil, for pan-frying
shredded scallion curls,
    to garnish

A popular delicacy found throughout many countries in the East, these crisp, golden fried toasts are very simple to make and perfect to serve with drinks at parties.

cook's tip

If you're catering for a party, it's a good idea to make the toasts in advance, then store them in the refrigerator or freezer. Cover and let chill for up to 3 days. Alternatively, place in a sealed container or plastic bag and freeze for up to 1 month. Thaw overnight in the refrigerator, then pop into a hot oven for 5 minutes to reheat thoroughly.

Place the chicken and shrimp in a food processor and process until very finely chopped. Add the egg, scallions, garlic, cilantro, fish sauce, pepper, and salt and pulse for a few seconds to mix well. Transfer to a large bowl.

Spread the mixture evenly over the slices of bread, right to the edges. Sprinkle the sesame seeds over a plate and press the spread side of each slice of bread into them to coat evenly.

Using a sharp knife, cut the bread into small rectangles, making 6 per slice.

Heat a 1/2-inch/1-cm depth of oil in a wide skillet until very hot. Pan-fry the bread rectangles quickly in batches for 2–3 minutes, or until golden brown, turning them over once.

Drain the toasts well on paper towels, transfer to a serving dish and garnish with shredded scallion curls. Serve hot.

thai **fish cakes** with

hot **peanut** dip

serves 4–5

15 minutes

15 minutes

12 oz/350 g skinless white fish fillet,
    such as cod or haddock
1 tbsp Thai fish sauce
2 tsp Thai red curry paste
1 tbsp lime juice
1 garlic clove, crushed
4 dried kaffir lime leaves, crumbled
1 egg white
3 tbsp chopped fresh cilantro
vegetable oil, for pan-frying

peanut dip

1 small fresh red chile
1 tbsp light soy sauce
1 tbsp lime juice
1 tbsp light brown sugar
3 tbsp chunky peanut butter
4 tbsp coconut milk
salt and pepper
snipped fresh chives, to garnish
salad greens, to serve

These little fish cakes are very popular in Thailand as street food, and make a perfect snack. Alternatively, serve them as an appetizer, complete with the spicy peanut dip.

Place the fish fillet in a food processor with the fish sauce, curry paste, lime juice, garlic, lime leaves, and egg white and process to a smooth paste.

Stir in the cilantro and quickly process again until mixed. Divide the mixture into 8–10 pieces and roll into balls, then flatten to make round patties. Set aside.

For the dip, halve and seed the chile, then chop finely. Place in a small pan with the remaining dip ingredients and heat gently, stirring constantly, until well blended. Adjust the seasoning to taste, if necessary, and transfer to a small bowl. Garnish with snipped chives and set aside until required.

Heat the oil for pan-frying in a wide skillet until very hot. Pan-fry the fish cakes in batches for 3–4 minutes on each side, until golden brown. Drain on paper towels and serve them hot on a bed of salad greens with the peanut dip.

steamed crab cakes

serves 4

25 minutes

20 minutes

1–2 banana leaves
2 garlic cloves, crushed
1 tsp finely chopped lemon grass
1/2 tsp pepper
2 tbsp chopped fresh cilantro
3 tbsp creamed coconut
1 tbsp lime juice
7 oz/200 g cooked crabmeat, flaked

1 tbsp Thai fish sauce
2 egg whites
1 egg yolk, lightly beaten
8 fresh cilantro leaves
corn oil, for deep-frying
chili dipping sauce, to serve

These pretty little steamed and deep-fried crab cakes are usually served as a snack, but you can serve them as an appetizer instead. In Thailand the banana leaves are skillfully shaped to make a container, but you can use ramekins, if you prefer.

Use the banana leaves to line 8 x 1/5-cup ramekins or foil containers.

Mix the garlic, lemon grass, pepper, and cilantro together in a bowl. Place the creamed coconut and lime juice in a separate bowl and mash until smooth. Stir the 2 mixtures together and add the crabmeat and fish sauce.

Whisk the egg whites in a clean, greasefree bowl until stiff, then lightly and evenly fold them into the crab mixture.

Spoon the mixture into the ramekins or foil containers lined with banana leaves and press down lightly. Brush the tops with egg yolk and top each with a cilantro leaf.

Place in a steamer half-filled with boiling water, then cover with a lid and let steam for 15 minutes, or until firm to the touch. Pour off the excess liquid and remove from the ramekins or foil containers.

Heat the oil for deep-frying in a large, heavy-bottom pan to 350°–375°F/180°–190°C, or until a cube of bread browns in 30 seconds. Add the crab cakes and deep-fry for 1 minute, turning them over once, until golden brown. Serve hot with a chili dipping sauce.

thai-style open crabmeat sandwich

serves 2

8 minutes

–

2 tbsp lime juice
3/4-inch/2-cm piece fresh gingerroot, grated
3/4-inch/2-cm piece lemon grass, finely chopped
5 tbsp mayonnaise
2 large slices crusty bread
1 ripe avocado

5 1/2 oz/150 g cooked crabmeat
pepper
fresh cilantro sprigs, to garnish
lime wedges, to serve

A hearty, open sandwich, topped with a classic flavor combination— crab with avocado and ginger. Perfect for a light summer lunch— or anytime!

cook's tip

To make homemade lime and ginger flavored mayonnaise, place 2 egg yolks, 1 tablespoon lime juice, and 1/2 teaspoon grated fresh gingerroot in a blender and blend briefly. With the motor running, gradually add 1 1/4 cups olive oil, drop by drop, until the mixture is thick and smooth. Season with salt and pepper.

Mix half the lime juice, ginger, and lemon grass together in a small bowl. Add the mayonnaise and mix well.

Spread 1 tablespoon of the mayonnaise smoothly over each slice of bread.

Halve the avocado and remove the pit. Peel and slice the flesh thinly, then arrange the slices on the bread. Sprinkle with a little of the remaining lime juice.

Spoon the crabmeat over the avocado, then add the remaining lime juice. Spoon over the remaining mayonnaise, season with pepper to taste, top with a cilantro sprig, and serve at once with lime wedges.

mussels
in spiced batter

serves 4

25 minutes

5 minutes

40 live large mussels in shells
2 tbsp all-purpose flour
2 tbsp rice flour
½ tsp salt
1 tbsp dry unsweetened coconut
1 egg white
1 tbsp rice wine or dry sherry

2 tbsp water
1 small fresh red Thai chile, seeded
　and chopped
1 tbsp chopped fresh cilantro
corn oil, for deep-frying
lime wedges, to serve

Little taste explosions—these make excellent nibbles to have with drinks before a meal, as they stimulate appetites, and leave everyone wanting more.

Wash the mussels thoroughly by scrubbing or scraping the shells and pulling out any beards that are attached to them. Discard any with broken shells or any that refuse to close when tapped. Place the mussels in a large pan with just the water that clings to their shells and cook, covered, over high heat for 2–3 minutes, shaking the pan occasionally, until the mussels open. Drain well, let cool slightly, then remove from the shells. Discard any mussels that remain closed.

For the batter, sift the all-purpose flour, rice flour, and salt into a large bowl. Add the coconut, egg white, rice wine, and water and beat until well mixed and a batter forms. Stir the chile and cilantro into the batter.

Heat a 2-inch/5-cm depth of oil for deep-frying in a large, heavy-bottom pan to 350°–375°F/180°–190°C, or until a cube of bread browns in 30 seconds. Holding the mussels with a fork, dip them quickly into the batter, then drop into the hot oil and deep-fry for 1–2 minutes, or until crisp and golden brown.

cook's tip

If you set the mussel shells aside, the cooked mussels can be replaced in them to serve.

Drain the mussels on paper towels and serve hot with lime wedges to squeeze over.

steamed mussels with lemon grass & basil

serves 4

15 minutes

5 minutes

2 lb 4 oz/1 kg live mussels in shells
2 shallots, finely chopped
1 lemon grass stalk, finely sliced
1 garlic clove, finely chopped
3 tbsp rice wine or dry sherry
2 tbsp lime juice
1 tbsp Thai fish sauce
4 tbsp chopped fresh basil

salt and pepper
2 tbsp butter
fresh basil leaves, to garnish
crusty bread, to serve

Thai cooks are fond of basil, and frequently sprinkle it over salads and soups. The familiar sweet basil available in Europe and America is ideal for use in most Thai recipes, including this one.

cook's tip

If you prefer to serve this dish as a main course, this amount will be enough for two portions. Fresh clams in shells are also very good when cooked by this method.

Wash the mussels thoroughly by scrubbing or scraping the shells and pulling out any beards that are attached to them. Discard any with broken shells or any that refuse to close when tapped.

Place the shallots, lemon grass, garlic, rice wine, lime juice, and fish sauce in a large, heavy-bottom pan and place over high heat.

Add the mussels, then cover and let steam for 2–3 minutes, shaking the pan occasionally, until the mussels open.

Discard any mussels that remain closed, then stir in the chopped basil and season to taste with salt and pepper.

Scoop out the mussels with a slotted spoon and divide between 4 deep bowls. Quickly whisk the butter into the pan juices, then pour the juices over the mussels.

Garnish each bowl with fresh basil leaves and serve with plenty of crusty bread to mop up the juices.

roasted spareribs
with honey & soy

serves 4

5 minutes

1 hour 10 minutes

2 lb 4 oz/1 kg Chinese-style
   spareribs
½ lemon
½ small orange
1-inch/2.5-cm piece fresh gingerroot
2 garlic cloves
1 small onion, chopped
2 tbsp soy sauce

2 tbsp rice wine or dry sherry
½ tsp Thai seven-spice powder
2 tbsp honey
1 tbsp sesame oil
lemon twists, to garnish
orange wedges, to serve

Ideally, ask your butcher to chop the spareribs into short lengths, about 2½ inches/6 cm long, so they're easy to eat with your fingers.

cook's tip

If you don't have a food processor, grate the rind and squeeze the juice from the citrus fruits. Grate the ginger, crush the garlic, and finely chop the onion. Mix these ingredients together with the remaining ingredients.

Preheat the oven to 350°F/180°C. Place the spareribs in a wide roasting pan, cover loosely with foil, and cook in the oven for 30 minutes.

Meanwhile, remove any seeds from the lemon and orange and place them in a food processor with the ginger, garlic, onion, soy sauce, rice wine, seven-spice powder, honey, and sesame oil. Process until smooth.

Increase the oven temperature to 400°F/200°C. Pour off any fat from the spareribs, then spoon the puréed mixture over the spareribs and toss to coat evenly.

Return the ribs to the oven and roast for 40 minutes, turning and basting them occasionally, until golden brown. Garnish with lemon twists and serve hot with orange wedges.

steamed
won ton bundles

serves 4

15 minutes

15–20 minutes

generous 1/2 cup cooked ground
  pork
1 tbsp dried shrimp, finely chopped
1 fresh green chile, finely chopped
2 shallots, finely chopped
1 tsp cornstarch
1 small egg, beaten
2 tsp dark soy sauce

2 tsp rice wine or dry sherry
salt and pepper
12 won ton skins
1 tsp sesame oil
chili dipping sauce, to serve

These little steamed dumplings are served as a first course with a spicy dip. It's worth making a large batch and keeping a few in the freezer to thaw and cook as you need them.

Mix the pork, dried shrimp, chile, and shallots together in a bowl. Blend the cornstarch with half the egg and stir into the pork mixture with the soy sauce and rice wine. Season to taste with salt and pepper.

Arrange the won ton skins flat on a clean counter and place 1 tablespoon of the pork mixture onto the center of each skin.

Brush the skins with the remaining egg and carefully pull up the edges, pinching together lightly at the top and leaving a small gap so the filling can just be seen.

Place enough water in the bottom of a steamer and bring to a boil. Brush the inside of the top part with sesame oil.

Arrange the won tons in the top, cover, and let steam for 15–20 minutes. Serve hot with a chili dipping sauce.

cook's tip

Make sure that the water in the bottom of the steamer is not allowed to go off the boil, otherwise the dumplings will be undercooked and soggy. Keep an eye on it to make sure that it doesn't boil dry—add extra boiling water if necessary.

crispy pork & peanut baskets

 serves 4

 10 minutes

 15 minutes

2 sheets phyllo pastry, about
    16½ x 11 inches/42 x 28 cm each
1 tbsp vegetable oil, plus extra
    for brushing
1 garlic clove, crushed
generous ½ cup cooked ground
    pork
1 tsp Thai red curry paste

2 scallions, finely chopped
3 tbsp crunchy peanut butter
1 tbsp light soy sauce
1 tbsp chopped fresh cilantro
salt and pepper
fresh cilantro sprigs, to garnish

*These tasty little appetite teasers
are an adaptation of a traditional
recipe that Thai cooks make with
a light batter, but phyllo pastry is a
good substitute that is much easier
to handle.*

cook's tip

*When using phyllo pastry,
remember that it dries out very
quickly and becomes brittle and
difficult to handle. Work quickly and
keep any sheets of pastry you're not
using covered with plastic wrap and
a dampened cloth.*

Preheat the oven to 400°F/200°C. Cut each sheet of phyllo pastry into 24 x 2¾-inch/7-cm squares, to make a total of 48 squares. Brush each square lightly with oil, and arrange the squares in stacks of 4 in 12 small muffin pans. Press the pastry down into the muffin pans.

Bake the pastry shells in the preheated oven for 6–8 minutes, or until golden brown.

Meanwhile, heat 1 tablespoon oil in a large, heavy-bottom skillet. Add the garlic and sauté for 30 seconds, then stir in the pork and stir-fry over high heat for 4–5 minutes, or until the meat is golden brown.

Add the curry paste and scallions and continue to stir-fry for an additional 1 minute, then stir in the peanut butter, soy sauce, and cilantro. Season to taste with salt and pepper.

Spoon the pork mixture into the phyllo baskets and serve hot, garnished with cilantro sprigs.

sticky ginger
chicken wings

serves 4

30 minutes,
plus 8 hours marinating

12–15 minutes

2 garlic cloves, coarsely chopped
1 piece preserved ginger in syrup,
    coarsely chopped
1 tsp coriander seeds
2 tbsp preserved ginger syrup
2 tbsp dark soy sauce
1 tbsp lime juice
1 tsp sesame oil
12 chicken wings

to garnish
lime wedges
fresh cilantro leaves

*A fingerlicking appetizer that's ideal
for parties. Have some finger bowls
and paper napkins ready.*

Place the garlic, preserved ginger, and coriander seeds in a mortar and
pestle and crush to a paste, gradually working in the ginger syrup, soy
sauce, lime juice, and sesame oil.

Tuck the pointed tip of each chicken wing underneath the thicker end of
the wing to make a neat triangular shape. Place in a large bowl.

Add the garlic and ginger paste to the bowl and toss the chicken wings in
the mixture to coat evenly. Cover and let marinate in the refrigerator for
several hours or overnight.

variation

*If you can't get chicken wings for
this recipe, use drumsticks instead,
but make sure that they are
thoroughly cooked before serving.*

Preheat the broiler to medium. Arrange the chicken in a single layer on a
foil-lined broiler pan and cook under the hot broiler for 12–15 minutes,
turning them occasionally, until golden brown and thoroughly cooked.

Alternatively, cook on a lightly oiled barbecue grill over medium hot coals.
Transfer to serving plates, garnish with lime wedges and cilantro leaves,
and serve at once.

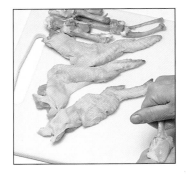

stuffed chicken wings

serves 4

25 minutes, plus
10–15 minutes soaking

40 minutes

8 chicken wings
3 tbsp dried shrimp
3 tbsp hot water
7/8 cup cooked ground pork
1 garlic clove, crushed
1 tbsp Thai fish sauce
1/2 tsp salt
1/2 tsp pepper
2 scallions, finely chopped

1/4 tsp ground turmeric
1 small egg, beaten
2 tbsp rice flour
corn oil, for deep-frying
fresh red chiles, to garnish

to serve

chili dipping sauce
cucumber, sliced

The preparation of this dish is time-consuming, but worth the effort. With their unusual, typically Thai, savory stuffing, the wings can be served hot or cold and make a delicious picnic dish.

Using a small sharp knife, cut round the end of the bone at the cut end of each wing, then loosen the flesh away from round the bone, scraping it downward with the knife and pulling back the skin as you go. When you reach the next joint, grasp the end of the bone, and twist sharply to break it at the joint. Remove the bone and turn back the flesh.

Continue to scrape the meat away down the length of the next long bone, exposing the joint. Twist to break the bone at the joint and remove, leaving just the wing tip in place.

Meanwhile, soak the dried shrimp in the hot water for 10–15 minutes. Drain, then chop. Place the pork, shrimp, garlic, fish sauce, salt, and pepper into a food processor and process to a smooth paste. Transfer to a bowl and add the scallions. Stir well. Use the mixture to stuff the chicken wings, pressing it down inside with your finger.

Beat the turmeric into the beaten egg and set aside. Dip each wing into the rice flour, shaking off the excess.

Heat a 2-inch/5-cm depth of oil in a large, heavy-bottom pan to 375°F/190°C, or until a cube of bread browns in 30 seconds. Dip the floured chicken wings quickly into the beaten egg, then drop carefully into the hot oil and deep-fry in small batches for 8–10 minutes, turning them over once. Drain the chicken wings on paper towels. Garnish with chiles and serve with cucumber slices and a chili dipping sauce.

lemon grass
chicken skewers

 serves 4

 30 minutes

 4–6 minutes

2 long or 4 short lemon grass stalks
2 large skinless, boneless chicken
   breasts, about 14 oz/400 g in total
1 small egg white
1 carrot, finely grated
1 small fresh red chile, seeded
   and chopped
2 tbsp snipped fresh garlic chives

2 tbsp chopped fresh cilantro
salt and pepper
1 tbsp corn oil

to garnish

fresh cilantro sprigs
lime slices
mixed salad greens, to serve

An unusual recipe in which fresh lemon grass stalks are used as skewers, which impart their delicate lemony flavor to the chicken mixture.

variation

If you can't find whole lemon grass stalks, you can use wooden or bamboo skewers instead, and add ¹/₂ teaspoon ground lemon grass to the mixture with the other flavorings.

If the lemon grass stalks are long, cut them in half across the center to make 4 short lengths. Cut each stalk in half lengthwise, so you have 8 sticks.

Coarsely chop the chicken pieces and place them in a food processor with the egg white. Process to a smooth paste, then add the carrot, chile, chives, cilantro, and salt and pepper. Process for a few seconds to mix well. Transfer the mixture to a large bowl, cover, and let chill in the refrigerator for 15 minutes.

Preheat the broiler to medium. Divide the mixture into 8 equal-size portions and use your hands to shape the mixture round the lemon grass "skewers."

Brush the chicken skewers with oil and cook under the hot broiler for 4–6 minutes, turning them occasionally, until golden brown and thoroughly cooked. Alternatively, barbecue over medium–hot coals.

Transfer to serving plates, garnish with cilantro sprigs and lime slices, and serve hot with salad greens.

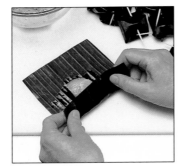

chicken fried in
banana leaves

serves 4–6

30 minutes,
plus 1 hour marinating

10–12 minutes

1 garlic clove, chopped
1 tsp finely chopped fresh gingerroot
¼ tsp pepper
2 fresh cilantro sprigs
1 tbsp Thai fish sauce
1 tbsp whiskey

3 skinless, boneless chicken breasts
2–3 banana leaves, cut into 3-inch/
    7.5-cm squares
corn oil, for pan-frying
chili dipping sauce, to serve

Leaves such as banana are often used in Thai cooking as a natural wrapping for all kinds of ingredients. These tasty little appetizers will set everyone's taste buds jumping.

cook's tip

To make a sweet chili dipping sauce to serve with the chicken pieces, mix together equal amounts of chili sauce and tomato ketchup, then stir in a dash of rice wine to taste.

Place the garlic, ginger, pepper, cilantro, fish sauce, and whiskey in a mortar and pestle and grind to a smooth paste.

Cut the chicken into 1-inch/2.5-cm chunks and toss in the paste to coat evenly. Cover and let marinate in the refrigerator for 1 hour.

Place a piece of chicken on a square of banana leaf and wrap it up like a package to enclose the chicken completely. Secure with wooden tooth-picks or tie with a piece of string.

Heat a ⅛-inch/3-mm depth of oil in a large, heavy-bottom skillet until hot.

Pan-fry the packages for 8–10 minutes, turning them over occasionally, until golden brown and the chicken is thoroughly cooked. Serve with a chili dipping sauce.

chicken balls with
dipping sauce

serves 4–6

10 minutes

25 minutes

2 large skinless, boneless chicken
  breasts
3 tbsp vegetable oil
2 shallots, finely chopped
½ celery stalk, finely chopped
1 garlic clove, crushed
2 tbsp light soy sauce
1 small egg, lightly beaten
salt and pepper
1 bunch of scallions
scallions tassels, to garnish

dipping sauce
3 tbsp dark soy sauce
1 tbsp rice wine or dry sherry
1 tsp sesame seeds

Serve these bite-size chicken appetizers warm as a snack, with drinks or packed cold for a picnic or lunch box treat.

Cut the chicken into ¾-inch/2-cm pieces. Heat half of the oil in a large skillet. Add the chicken and stir-fry over high heat for 2–3 minutes, until golden. Remove the chicken with a slotted spoon and set aside.

Add the shallots, celery, and garlic to the skillet and stir-fry for 1–2 minutes, or until softened but not browned.

Place the chicken, shallots, celery, and garlic in a food processor and process until finely ground. Add 1 tablespoon of the light soy sauce, just enough egg to make a fairly firm mixture and salt and pepper.

Trim the scallions and cut into 2-inch/5-cm lengths. Set aside until required. Make the dipping sauce by mixing the dark soy sauce, rice wine, and sesame seeds together in a bowl. Set aside.

Form the chicken mixture into 16–18 walnut-size balls between the palms of your hands. Heat the remaining oil in the skillet and stir-fry the balls in small batches for 4–5 minutes, or until golden brown. As each batch is cooked, drain on paper towels and keep hot.

Stir-fry the reserved scallions for 1–2 minutes, until they start to soften, then stir in the remaining light soy sauce. Serve with the chicken balls and dipping sauce, garnished with scallion tassels.

stuffed eggs with pork & crabmeat

serves 4

15 minutes

15 minutes

4 large eggs
scant ½ cup cooked ground pork
6 oz/175 g canned white crabmeat,
  drained
1 garlic clove, crushed
1 tsp Thai fish sauce
½ tsp ground lemon grass
1 tbsp chopped fresh cilantro
1 tbsp dry unsweetened coconut

salt and pepper
generous ⅔ cup all-purpose flour
about ⅔ cup coconut milk
corn oil, for deep-frying
green salad, to serve
cucumber flowers, to garnish

These savory stuffed eggs make a good picnic dish, or they can be popped into a lunch box for an unusual treat. Cool the eggs completely before packing.

Place the eggs in a pan of simmering water and bring to a boil, then let simmer for 10 minutes. Drain the eggs, crack the shells, and let cool under cold running water. Remove the shells.

Cut the eggs lengthwise down the center and scoop out the yolks. Place the yolks in a bowl with the pork, crabmeat, garlic, fish sauce, lemon grass, cilantro, and coconut. Season to taste with salt and pepper and mix well.

Divide the mixture into 8 equal portions, then fill each of the egg whites with the mixture, pressing together with your hands to form the shape of a whole egg.

Whisk the flour and enough coconut milk together to make a thick coating batter, seasoning with salt and pepper.

Heat a 2-inch/5-cm depth of oil in a large, heavy-bottom pan to 375°F/190°C, or until a cube of bread browns in 30 seconds. Dip each egg into the coconut batter, then shake off the excess.

Deep-fry the eggs in 2 batches for 5 minutes, turning occasionally, until golden brown. Remove with a slotted spoon and drain on paper towels. Serve warm or cold with a green salad garnished with cucumber flowers.

thai stuffed omelet

serves 4

5–10 minutes

25 minutes

2 garlic cloves, chopped
4 black peppercorns
4 fresh cilantro sprigs
2 tbsp vegetable oil
7/8 cup cooked ground pork
2 scallions, chopped
1 large, firm tomato, chopped
6 large eggs

1 tbsp Thai fish sauce
1/4 tsp ground turmeric
mixed salad greens, tossed, to serve

This makes a substantial appetizer, or a light lunch or supper dish. Serve with a colorful, crisp salad to accompany the dish.

cook's tip

If you prefer, spread half the pork mixture evenly over one omelet, then place a second omelet on top, without folding. Cut into slim wedges to serve.

Place the garlic, peppercorns, and cilantro in a mortar and, using a pestle, crush to a smooth paste.

Heat 1 tablespoon of the oil in a large skillet over medium heat. Add the paste and sauté for 1–2 minutes, until it just changes color.

Stir in the pork and stir-fry until it is lightly browned. Add the scallions and tomato, and stir-fry for an additional 1 minute, then remove the skillet from the heat.

Heat the remaining oil in a small, heavy-bottom skillet. Beat the eggs with the fish sauce and turmeric, then pour one-quarter of the egg mixture into the skillet. As the mixture starts to set, stir lightly to ensure that all the liquid egg is set.

Spoon one-quarter of the pork mixture down the center of the omelet, then fold the sides inward toward the center, enclosing the filling. Make 3 more omelets with the remaining egg and fill with the remaining pork mixture.

Slide the omelets onto serving plates and serve with salad greens.

vegetarian
egg rolls

serves 4

20 minutes

20 minutes

1 oz/25 g fine cellophane noodles
2 tbsp peanut oil, plus extra for
   deep-frying
2 garlic cloves, crushed
1/2 tsp grated fresh gingerroot
2 oz/55 g oyster mushrooms,
   thinly sliced
2 scallions, finely chopped
scant 1 cup bean sprouts
1 small carrot, finely shredded
1/2 tsp sesame oil

1 tbsp light soy sauce
1 tbsp rice wine or dry sherry
1/4 tsp pepper
1 tbsp chopped fresh cilantro
1 tbsp chopped fresh mint
24 egg roll skins
1/2 tsp cornstarch
1 fresh mint sprig, to garnish
chili dipping sauce, to serve

These bite-size vegetarian noodle-filled rolls are a tasty appetizer to serve at the start of any meal with a chili dipping sauce.

Place the noodles in a heatproof bowl, pour over enough boiling water to cover, and let stand for 4 minutes. Drain, rinse in cold water, then drain again. Use sharp knife to cut into 2-inch/5-cm lengths.

Heat the oil in a preheated wok or wide skillet over high heat. Add the garlic, ginger, oyster mushrooms, scallions, bean sprouts, and carrot and stir-fry for 1 minute, or until just softened.

Stir in the sesame oil, soy sauce, rice wine, pepper, cilantro, and mint, then remove the skillet from the heat. Stir in the rice noodles.

Arrange the egg roll skins on a counter, pointing diagonally. Mix the cornstarch with 1 tablespoon water in a small bowl and use to brush the edges of 1 skin. Spoon a little filling onto the pointed side of the same skin.

Roll the point of the skin over the filling, then fold the side points inward over the filling. Continue to roll up the skin away from you, moistening the tip with more cornstarch mixture to secure the roll. Make up all the egg rolls in the same way.

Heat the oil for deep-frying in a wok or deep skillet to 350°F/180°C, or until a cube of bread browns in 30 seconds. Add the rolls in batches and deep-fry for 2–3 minutes each, until golden brown and crisp. Drain and transfer to a plate. Garnish with mint and serve with a dipping sauce.

sweet & sour

seafood salad

serves 6

20 minutes

10 minutes

18 live mussels in shells
6 large scallops
7 oz/200 g baby squid, cleaned
2 shallots, finely chopped
6 raw jumbo shrimp, shelled and
    deveined
1/4 cucumber
1 carrot
1/4 head napa cabbage, shredded

dressing

4 tbsp lime juice
2 garlic cloves, finely chopped
2 tbsp Thai fish sauce
1 tsp sesame oil
1 tbsp light brown sugar
2 tbsp chopped fresh mint
1/2 tsp pepper
salt

This unusual seafood dish with a sweet lime dressing can be an appetizer or doubled up for a buffet-style main dish. It is also a good dish to prepare for a crowd if you are entertaining.

Wash the mussels thoroughly by scrubbing or scraping the shells and pulling out any beards that are attached to them. Discard any with broken shells and any that refuse to close when tapped. Place the remaining mussels in a large pan with just the water that clings to their shells and cook, covered, for 1–2 minutes, until they have opened. Remove with a slotted spoon, reserving the liquid in the pan. Discard any mussels that remain closed.

Using a sharp knife, separate the corals from the scallops, then cut the white parts in half horizontally. Cut the tentacles from the squid and slice the body cavities into rings.

Add the shallots to the liquid in the pan and let simmer over high heat until the liquid is reduced to 3 tablespoons. Add the scallops, squid, and jumbo shrimp and stir for 2–3 minutes, until cooked. Remove the pan from the heat and transfer the mixture to a wide bowl. Add the mussels.

Cut the cucumber and carrot in half lengthwise, then slice thinly on a diagonal angle to make long, pointed slices. Toss with the napa cabbage.

To make the dressing, place all the ingredients in a screw-top jar and shake well until evenly combined. Season with salt to taste.

Add the vegetables to the seafood in the bowl and toss together. Spoon the dressing over and serve at once.

warm salad of tuna & tomatoes
with ginger dressing

 serves 4

 15 minutes

 8 minutes

1³/4 oz/50 g napa cabbage, shredded
3 tbsp rice wine or dry sherry
2 tbsp Thai fish sauce
1 tbsp finely shredded fresh
   gingerroot
1 garlic clove, finely chopped
¹/2 small fresh red Thai chile,
   finely chopped

2 tsp light brown sugar
2 tbsp lime juice
14 oz/400 g fresh tuna steak
corn oil, for brushing
4¹/2 oz/125 g cherry tomatoes, cut
   into halves
fresh mint leaves and mint sprigs,
   coarsely chopped, to garnish

A colorful, refreshing first course that is perfect to make for a special summer lunch or dinner. The dressing can be made in advance and spooned over the dish just before serving.

variation

You can make a quick version of this dish using canned tuna. Just drain and flake the tuna, add with the tomatoes to the skillet, and cook until the tomatoes are lightly browned. Continue as in the recipe.

Place a small pile of shredded napa cabbage on a serving plate. Place the rice wine, fish sauce, ginger, garlic, chile, brown sugar, and 1 tablespoon lime juice in a screw-top jar and shake well to combine evenly.

Using a sharp knife, cut the tuna into strips of an even thickness. Sprinkle with the remaining lime juice.

Brush a wide skillet or ridged griddle with oil and heat until very hot. Arrange the tuna strips in the skillet and cook until just firm and light golden, turning them over once. Remove the tuna from the skillet and set aside.

Add the tomatoes to the skillet and cook over high heat until lightly browned. Spoon the tuna and tomatoes over the napa cabbage, then spoon over the dressing. Garnish with fresh mint and serve warm.

chile-spiced shrimp won ton soup

serves 4

20 minutes

5 minutes

won tons

6 oz/175 g cooked shelled shrimp
1 garlic clove, crushed
1 scallion, finely chopped
1 tbsp dark soy sauce
1 tbsp Thai fish sauce
1 tbsp chopped fresh cilantro
1 small egg, separated
12 won ton skins

soup

2 small fresh red Thai chiles
2 scallions
4 cups clear beef stock
1 tbsp Thai fish sauce
1 tbsp dark soy sauce
1 tbsp rice wine or dry sherry
handful of fresh cilantro leaves,
    to garnish

This delicious soup has a real kick of red-hot chiles, perfect to warm up a winter's day. If you prefer a milder flavor, remove the seeds from the chiles before using them.

Finely chop the shrimp. Place them in a bowl and stir in the garlic, scallion, soy sauce, fish sauce, cilantro, and egg yolk.

Lay the won ton skins on a counter in a single layer and place about 1 tablespoon of the filling mixture in the center of each. Brush the edges with egg white and fold each one into a triangle, pressing lightly to seal. Bring the 2 bottom corners of the triangle around to meet in the center, securing with a little egg white to hold in place.

For the soup, slice the chiles at a steep diagonal angle to make long thin slices. Slice the scallions on the same angle.

Place the stock, fish sauce, soy sauce, and rice wine in a large pan and bring to a boil. Add the chiles and scallions. Drop the won tons into the pan and let simmer for 4–5 minutes, until thoroughly heated.

Serve the soup and won tons in small bowls. Garnish with fresh cilantro leaves sprinkled over at the last moment.

hot & sour soup

serves 4

15 minutes

30 minutes

12 oz/350 g whole raw or cooked
   shrimp in shells
1 tbsp vegetable oil
1 lemon grass stalk, coarsely chopped
2 kaffir lime leaves, shredded
1 fresh green chile, seeded and
   chopped
5 cups chicken or fish stock
1 lime

1 tbsp Thai fish sauce
salt and pepper
1 fresh red Thai chile, seeded and
   thinly sliced
1 scallion, thinly sliced
1 tbsp finely chopped fresh cilantro,
   to garnish

*Hot and sour mixtures are popular
throughout the East, especially in
Thailand. This soup typically has
either shrimp or chicken added, but
tofu can be used instead if you
prefer a meatless version.*

cook's tip

*To devein the shrimp, remove the
shells. Cut a slit along the back of
each shrimp and remove the fine
black vein that runs along the
length of the back. Wipe with
paper towels.*

Shell the shrimp and set the shells aside. Devein the shrimp (see Cook's
Tip), then cover with plastic wrap and let chill in the refrigerator.

Heat the oil in a large, heavy-bottom pan. Add the shrimp shells and stir-
fry for 3–4 minutes, or until they turn pink. Add the lemon grass, lime
leaves, chile, and stock. Pare a thin strip of zest from the lime and grate the
rest. Add the grated rind to the pan.

Bring to a boil, then lower the heat, cover, and let simmer for 20 minutes.

Strain the liquid and pour it back into the pan. Squeeze the juice from the
lime and add to the pan with the fish sauce and salt and pepper to taste.

Bring to a boil, then lower the heat and add the shrimp. Let simmer for
2–3 minutes.

Add the thinly sliced chile and scallion. Sprinkle with the chopped cilantro
and serve at once.

creamy corn soup with egg

serves 4

5–10 minutes

15–20 minutes

1 tbsp vegetable oil
3 garlic cloves, crushed
1 tsp grated fresh gingerroot
3 cups chicken stock
13 oz/375 g canned creamed corn
1 tbsp Thai fish sauce
6 oz/175 g canned white crabmeat, drained

salt and pepper
1 egg

to garnish

fresh cilantro, shredded
paprika

This speedy soup is a good pantry standby, made in a matter of minutes. If you prefer, you can use frozen crab sticks, thawed and chopped, or cooked shrimp instead of canned crabmeat.

variation

To give the soup an extra rich flavor kick for a special occasion, stir in 1 tablespoon of rice wine or dry sherry just before you ladle it into bowls.

Heat the oil in a large, heavy-bottom pan. Add the garlic and sauté for 1 minute, stirring constantly.

Add the ginger to the pan, then stir in the stock and creamed corn. Bring to a boil.

Stir in the fish sauce, crabmeat, and add salt and pepper, to taste. Return the soup to a boil.

Beat the egg in a small bowl, then stir lightly into the soup so it sets into long strands. Let simmer gently for 30 seconds, or until just set.

Ladle the soup into serving bowls and serve hot, garnished with shredded cilantro and paprika sprinkled over.

pumpkin &
coconut soup

serves 6

15 minutes

40 minutes

2 lb 4 oz/1 kg pumpkin
1 tbsp peanut oil
1 tsp yellow mustard seeds
1 garlic clove, crushed
1 large onion, chopped
1 celery stalk, chopped
1 small fresh red chile, chopped
3 1/2 cups stock

1 tbsp dried shrimp
5 tbsp coconut cream
salt and pepper

This substantial soup is filling and, if served with crusty bread, is all you need for a satisfying lunch. For a first course, serve in small bowls with a spoonful of spicy relish stirred into each portion.

cook's tip

For an extra touch of garnish, swirl a spoonful of thick coconut milk into each bowl of soup as you serve it.

Using a sharp knife, halve the pumpkin and remove the seeds. Cut away the skin and dice the flesh.

Heat the oil in a large, ovenproof casserole. Add the mustard seeds and sauté until they start to pop. Stir in the garlic, onion, celery, and chile, and stir-fry for 1–2 minutes.

Add the pumpkin with the stock and dried shrimp to the casserole and bring to a boil. Lower the heat, cover, and let simmer for 30 minutes, or until the ingredients are very tender.

Transfer the mixture to a food processor or blender and process until smooth. Return to the casserole and stir in the coconut cream.

Season to taste with salt and pepper and serve hot.

mushroom

& tofu broth

serves 4

35 minutes

15 minutes

4 dried black mushrooms
1 tbsp corn oil
1 tsp sesame oil
1 garlic clove, crushed
1 fresh green chile, seeded and
   finely chopped
6 scallions, sliced
3 oz/85 g fresh oyster mushrooms,
   sliced

2 fresh kaffir lime leaves, finely
   shredded
4 cups rich brown stock
2 tbsp lime juice
1 tbsp rice vinegar or white
   wine vinegar
1 tbsp Thai fish sauce
3 oz/85 g firm tofu, diced
   (drained weight)
salt and pepper

*Combining different types of
mushrooms and tofu, this delicious
soup is incredibly easy to make.
Serve as part of a dinner party
menu or as a light lunch.*

cook's tip

*Use a clear, richly colored
homemade beef stock, or a
Japanese dashi, to make an
attractive clear broth. Bouillon cubes
generally make a cloudy stock. To
make a vegetarian version of the
broth, use a well-flavored vegetable
stock and replace the fish sauce
with light soy sauce.*

Pour 1/3 cup boiling water over the dried black mushrooms in a heatproof
bowl and let soak for 30 minutes. Drain, reserving the liquid, then chop the
black mushrooms coarsely

Heat the corn and sesame oils in a large pan or preheated wok over high
heat. Add the garlic, chile, and scallions and stir-fry for 1 minute, until
softened but not browned.

Add all of the mushrooms, kaffir lime leaves, stock, and reserved mushroom liquid. Bring to a boil.

Stir in the lime juice, rice vinegar, and fish sauce, then lower the heat and
let simmer gently for 3–4 minutes.

Add the diced tofu and season to taste with salt and pepper. Heat gently
until boiling, then serve at once.

rice soup with eggs

serves 4

5 minutes

10 minutes

1 tsp corn oil	3 cup cooked long-grain rice
1 garlic clove, crushed	1 tbsp Thai fish sauce
scant ¼ cup cooked ground pork	salt and pepper
3 scallions, sliced	4 small eggs
1 tbsp grated fresh gingerroot	2 tbsp shredded fresh cilantro,
1 fresh red Thai chile, seeded and	to garnish
chopped	
4 cups chicken stock	

This version of a classic Thai soup, sometimes eaten for breakfast, is a good way of using up any leftover cooked rice, especially when you've cooked too much.

cook's tip

If you prefer, beat the eggs together and cook like an omelet until set, then cut into ribbonlike strips and add to the soup just before serving.

Heat the oil in a large pan or preheated wok. Add the garlic and pork and stir-fry gently for 1 minute, or until the meat is broken up but not browned.

Stir in the scallions, ginger, chile, and stock, stirring until boiling. Add the rice, lower the heat, and let simmer for 2 minutes.

Add the fish sauce and season to taste with salt and pepper. Carefully break the eggs into the soup and let simmer over very low heat for 3–4 minutes, or until set.

Ladle the soup into large bowls, allowing 1 egg per portion. Garnish with shredded cilantro and serve at once.

spinach & ginger soup

serves 4

5–10 minutes

25 minutes

2 tbsp corn oil
I onion, chopped
2 garlic cloves, finely chopped
I-inch/2.5-cm piece fresh gingerroot,
   finely chopped
6 cups fresh young spinach leaves
I small lemon grass stalk, finely
   chopped

4 cups chicken or vegetable stock
I small potato, chopped
I tbsp rice wine or dry sherry
salt and pepper
I tsp sesame oil

This mildly spiced, rich green soup is delicately scented with ginger and lemon grass. It makes a good light appetizer or summer lunch dish.

variation

To make a creamy textured spinach and coconut soup, stir in 4 tablespoons creamed coconut, or alternatively replace 1¼ cups of the stock with coconut milk. Serve the soup with shavings of fresh coconut sprinkled over the surface.

Heat the oil in a large pan. Add the onion, garlic, and ginger and stir-fry gently for 3–4 minutes, until softened but not browned.

Set aside 2–3 small spinach leaves. Add the remaining leaves and lemon grass to the pan, stirring until the spinach is wilted. Add the stock and potato to the pan and bring to a boil. Lower the heat, cover, and let simmer for 10 minutes.

Transfer the soup to a food processor or blender and process until completely smooth.

Return the soup to the pan and add the rice wine, then adjust the seasoning to taste with salt and pepper. Heat until just about to boil.

Finely shred the reserved spinach leaves and sprinkle some over the top. Drizzle with a few drops of sesame oil and serve hot, garnished with the remaining finely shredded spinach leaves.

chilled avocado, lime
& cilantro soup

serves 4

15 minutes

–

2 ripe avocados
1 small mild onion, chopped
1 garlic clove, crushed
2 tbsp chopped fresh cilantro
1 tbsp chopped fresh mint
2 tbsp lime juice
3 cups vegetable stock
1 tbsp rice vinegar or white
  wine vinegar
1 tbsp light soy sauce
salt and pepper

to garnish

2 tbsp sour cream
1 tbsp finely chopped fresh cilantro
2 tsp lime juice
finely shredded lime rind

A delightfully simple soup with a blend of typical Thai flavors, which needs no cooking and can be served at any time of day.

cook's tip

The top surface of the soup may darken slightly if the soup is stored for longer than 1 hour, but don't worry—just give it a quick stir before serving. If you plan to keep the soup for several hours, cover the surface with a piece of plastic wrap.

Halve, pit, and scoop out the flesh from the avocados. Place in a food processor or blender with the onion, garlic, cilantro, mint, lime juice, and about half the stock and process until completely smooth.

Add the remaining stock, rice vinegar, and soy sauce and process again to mix well. Taste and adjust the seasoning if necessary, or add a little extra lime juice if required. Cover and let chill in the refrigerator until required.

To make the lime and cilantro cream garnish, mix the sour cream, cilantro, and lime juice together in a small bowl. Spoon into the soup just before serving and sprinkle with shredded lime rind.

meat & fish main dishes

The Thais are primarily a fish-eating nation, and meat features less in most meals, except for special celebrations. The waterways of Thailand are teeming with many types of fish—even in the channels between the rice paddy fields—and the warm seas bring an abundance of fish and shellfish.

Even in the heart of Bangkok city, the markets are packed with fresh fish and seafood of all kinds. In Thai coastal towns, rows of thatch-roofed beach kiosks sell every type of fresh seafood from the warm Gulf waters—from barbecued or sautéed fish with ginger, to shrimp in coconut milk and cilantro—to locals and visitors alike.

Because of the Thai Buddhist religion, which forbids the killing of animals, most butchers are immigrant workers. Religion does not forbid eating meat, though it is often regarded as a special treat. Chicken is much more common than beef, and it's not unusual to see chicken, or sometimes pork, combined with seafood such as shrimp or crabmeat—a combination which works surprisingly well. Duck, another Thai favorite, is frequently barbecue-roasted with warm spices and soy or sweet glazes, much as in the Chinese style.

stir-fried beef with bean sprouts

serves 4

5 minutes

15 minutes

1 bunch of scallions
2 tbsp corn oil
1 garlic clove, crushed
1 tsp finely chopped fresh gingerroot
1 lb 2 oz/500 g tender beef, cut into
   thin strips
1 large red bell pepper, seeded
   and sliced
1 small fresh red chile, seeded
   and chopped
2 1/4 cups fresh bean sprouts

1 small lemon grass stalk, finely
   chopped
2 tbsp smooth peanut butter
4 tbsp coconut milk
1 tbsp rice vinegar or white
   wine vinegar
1 tbsp soy sauce
1 tsp light brown sugar
9 oz/250 g medium egg noodles
salt and pepper

A quick and easy stir-fry for any day of the week, this simple beef recipe makes a good main dish. Serve with a green salad, if you like.

Thinly slice the scallions, reserving some slices to use as a garnish.

Heat the oil in a skillet or preheated wok over high heat. Add the scallions, garlic, and ginger and stir-fry for 2–3 minutes to soften. Add the beef and continue stir-frying for 4–5 minutes, until evenly browned.

Add the bell pepper and stir-fry for an additional 3–4 minutes. Add the chile and bean sprouts and stir-fry for 2 minutes. Mix the lemon grass, peanut butter, coconut milk, rice vinegar, soy sauce, and sugar together in a bowl, then stir into the skillet.

Meanwhile, cook the egg noodles in boiling salted water for 4 minutes, or according to the package instructions. Drain and stir into the skillet, tossing to mix evenly.

Season to taste with salt and pepper. Sprinkle with the reserved scallions and serve hot.

beef satay with peanut sauce

serves 4

2 hours 15 minutes

15 minutes

1 lb 2 oz/500 g beef fillet
2 garlic cloves, crushed
3/4-inch/2-cm piece fresh gingerroot, finely grated
1 tbsp light brown sugar
1 tbsp dark soy sauce
1 tbsp lime juice
2 tsp sesame oil
1 tsp ground coriander
1 tsp ground turmeric
1/2 tsp chili powder

peanut sauce

1 1/4 cups coconut milk
8 tbsp crunchy peanut butter
1/2 small onion, grated
2 tsp light brown sugar
1/2 tsp chili powder
1 tbsp dark soy sauce

to garnish

chopped cucumber
red bell pepper pieces

Satay recipes vary throughout the East, but these little beef skewers are a classic version of the traditional dish. The deliciously moreish peanut sauce turns the skewers into a rich, substantial dish.

cook's tip

Make sure the broiler or barbecue is very hot before you start to cook. Soak the skewers in cold water for 20 minutes before using to reduce the risk of the skewers burning. For an elegant presentation, serve the sauce in a large lettuce leaf, garnished with snipped fresh chives.

Cut the beef into 1/2-inch/1-cm cubes and place in a large bowl.

Add the garlic, ginger, sugar, soy sauce, lime juice, sesame oil, ground coriander, turmeric, and chili powder. Mix well to coat the pieces of meat evenly. Cover and let marinate in the refrigerator for at least 2 hours or overnight.

Preheat the broiler to high. To make the peanut sauce, place all the ingredients in a pan and stir over medium heat until boiling. Remove the pan from the heat and keep warm.

Thread the beef cubes onto presoaked bamboo skewers. Cook the beef skewers under the hot broiler for 3–5 minutes, turning frequently, until golden. Alternatively, barbecue over hot coals. Transfer to a large serving plate, garnish with chopped cucumber and red bell pepper pieces, and serve with the peanut sauce.

beef & bell peppers with
lemon grass

serves 4

5 minutes

8 minutes

1 lb 2 oz/500 g lean beef fillet
2 tbsp vegetable oil
1 garlic clove, finely chopped
1 lemon grass stalk, finely shredded
1-inch/2.5-cm piece fresh gingerroot, finely chopped
1 red bell pepper, seeded and thickly sliced

1 green bell pepper, seeded and thickly sliced
1 onion, thickly sliced
2 tbsp lime juice
salt and pepper
freshly cooked noodles or rice, to serve

A delicately flavored stir-fry infused with lemon grass and ginger. Colorful bell peppers help to complete the dish, and it's all cooked within a matter of minutes!

cook's tip

When preparing lemon grass, take care to remove the outer layers, which can be tough and fibrous. Use only the center, tender part, which has the finest flavor.

Cut the beef into long, thin strips, cutting across the grain.

Heat the oil in a large skillet or preheated wok over high heat. Add the garlic and stir-fry for 1 minute.

Add the beef and stir-fry for an additional 2–3 minutes, or until lightly colored. Stir in the lemon grass and ginger and remove the skillet from the heat.

Remove the beef from the skillet and keep to one side. Next add the bell peppers and onion to the skillet and stir-fry over high heat for 2–3 minutes, or until the onions are just turning golden brown and slightly softened.

Return the beef to the skillet, stir in the lime juice, and season to taste with salt and pepper. Stir-fry over high heat for 1–2 minutes to heat through. Serve with freshly cooked noodles or rice.

red-hot beef
with cashews

serves 4

2–3 hours 15 minutes

10 minutes

1 lb 2 oz/500 g lean, boneless
  beef sirloin
1 tsp vegetable oil

marinade

1 tbsp sesame seeds
1 garlic clove, chopped
1 tbsp finely chopped fresh
  gingerroot
1 fresh red Thai chile, chopped
2 tbsp dark soy sauce
1 tsp Thai red curry paste

to finish

1 tsp sesame oil
4 tbsp unsalted cashews
1 scallion, thickly sliced diagonally
cucumber slices, to garnish

Hot and spicy, these quick-cooked beef strips are very tempting. Serve them with lots of plain rice and cucumber slices to offset the heat.

Using a sharp knife, cut the beef into ½-inch/1-cm wide strips. Place them in a large, nonmetallic bowl.

To make the marinade, toast the sesame seeds in a heavy-bottom skillet over medium heat for 2–3 minutes, until golden brown, shaking the skillet occasionally.

Place the seeds in a mortar and pestle with the garlic, ginger, and chile, and grind to a smooth paste. Add the soy sauce and curry paste and mix well.

Spoon the paste over the beef strips and toss to coat the meat evenly. Cover and let marinate in the refrigerator for at least 2–3 hours or overnight.

Heat a heavy-bottom skillet or ridged griddle until very hot and brush with vegetable oil. Place the beef strips in the skillet and cook quickly, turning frequently, until lightly browned. Remove the skillet from the heat and spoon the beef into a pile on a hot serving dish.

Heat the sesame oil in a small skillet. Add the cashews and quickly sauté until golden. Add the scallion and stir-fry for 30 seconds. Sprinkle the mixture on top of the beef strips, garnish with cucumber slices, and serve at once.

hot beef &
coconut curry

serves 4

10 minutes

45 minutes

1³⁄₄ cups coconut milk
2 tbsp Thai red curry paste
2 garlic cloves, crushed
1 lb 2 oz/500 g braising steak
2 fresh kaffir lime leaves, shredded
3 tbsp lime juice
2 tbsp Thai fish sauce
1 large fresh red chile, seeded
  and sliced

¹⁄₂ tsp ground turmeric
salt and pepper
2 tbsp chopped fresh basil leaves
2 tbsp chopped fresh cilantro leaves
shredded coconut, to garnish
freshly cooked rice, to serve

The heat of the chiles in this red-hot curry is balanced and softened by the coconut milk, producing a creamy textured, rich and lavishly spiced dish.

cook's tip

This recipe uses one of the larger, milder red chile peppers—either fresno or Dutch—simply because they give more color to the dish. If you prefer to use small Thai chiles, you'll need only one because they are much hotter.

For an elegant presentation, garnish the rice with a few strips of fresh red chile.

Place the coconut milk in a large pan and bring to a boil. Lower the heat and let simmer gently for 10 minutes, until the milk has thickened. Stir in the curry paste and garlic and let simmer for an additional 5 minutes.

Cut the beef into ³⁄₄-inch/2-cm chunks. Add to the pan and bring to a boil, stirring constantly. Lower the heat and add the lime leaves, lime juice, fish sauce, chile, turmeric, and ¹⁄₂ teaspoon salt.

Cover the pan and continue simmering for 20–25 minutes, or until the meat is tender, adding a little water if the sauce looks too dry.

Stir in the basil and cilantro and season to taste with salt and pepper. Sprinkle with shredded coconut and serve with freshly cooked rice.

 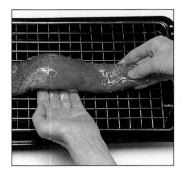 

roasted red pork

serves 4

15 minutes,
plus 8 hours marinating

1 hour

1 lb 5 oz/600 g pork fillets
napa cabbage, shredded, to serve
1 fresh red chile flower, to garnish

marinade

2 garlic cloves, crushed
1 tbsp grated fresh gingerroot
1 tbsp light soy sauce
1 tbsp Thai fish sauce

1 tbsp rice wine or dry sherry
1 tbsp hoisin sauce
1 tbsp sesame oil
1 tbsp jaggery or soft
  brown sugar
1/2 tsp Chinese five-spice powder
few drops red food coloring
  (optional)

This red-glazed, sweet and tender pork, of Chinese origin, is a colorful addition to many stir-fries, salads, and soups. Alternatively, simply serve it sliced and arranged on a bed of napa cabbage.

variation

The pork may also be broiled. Cut the meat into slices or strips and coat in the marinade, then arrange on a foil-lined broiler pan and broil under high heat, turning occasionally and basting with marinade.

Mix all the ingredients for the marinade together in a small bowl, then spread over the pork, turning to coat evenly. Place in a large dish, cover, and let marinate in the refrigerator overnight.

Preheat the oven to 425°F/220°C. Place a rack in a roasting pan, then half-fill the pan with boiling water. Lift the pork from the marinade and place on the rack. Set aside the marinade.

Roast the pork in the preheated oven for 20 minutes. Baste with the marinade, then lower the heat to 350°F/180°C and continue roasting for an additional 35–40 minutes, basting occasionally with the marinade, until the pork is a rich reddish brown and thoroughly cooked.

Cut the pork into slices and serve on a bed of shredded napa cabbage, garnished with a red chile flower.

pork with
soy & sesame glaze

serves 4

40 minutes

35 minutes

2 pork fillets, about
  9½ oz/275 g each
2 tbsp dark soy sauce
2 tbsp honey
2 garlic cloves, crushed

1 tbsp sesame seeds
1 onion, thinly sliced in rings
1 tbsp all-purpose flour, seasoned
corn oil, for cooking
crisp salad greens, to serve

Thai cooks are fond of adding sweet flavors to meat, as in this unusual pork dish, with soy and garlic to balance the sweetness of the honey. Pork fillet is a very lean meat, so take care not to overcook it otherwise it will become dry.

cook's tip

This pork is also excellent served cold, and it's a good choice for picnics, especially served with Chile & Coconut Sambal (see page 162) or chili relish.

Preheat the oven to 400°F/200°C. Trim the pork fillets and place in a wide, nonmetallic dish.

Mix the soy sauce, honey, and garlic together in a small bowl, then spread over the pork, turning to coat evenly.

Lift the pork fillets into a roasting pan or shallow ovenproof dish and sprinkle evenly with sesame seeds.

Roast the pork in the preheated oven for 20 minutes, spooning over any juices. Cover loosely with foil to prevent overbrowning and roast for an additional 10–15 minutes, or until the meat is thoroughly cooked.

Meanwhile, dip the onion slices in the seasoned flour and shake off the excess. Heat the oil in a small skillet. Add the onion rings and cook until golden and crisp, turning occasionally. Serve the pork in slices with the cooked onions on a bed of crisp salad greens.

stir-fried
pork & corn

serves 4

2 minutes

8–10 minutes

2 tbsp vegetable oil
1 lb 2 oz/500 g lean boneless pork,
  cut in thin strips
1 garlic clove, chopped
3 cups fresh corn kernels
7 oz/200 g green beans, cut into
  short lengths
2 scallions, chopped

1 small fresh red chile, chopped
1 tsp sugar
1 tbsp light soy sauce
3 tbsp chopped fresh cilantro
freshly cooked egg noodles or rice,
  to serve

A speedy dish, typical of Thai street food. This includes fresh corn, which, although introduced relatively recently to Thailand, is a very popular vegetable used in many dishes. Fresh corn from the cob, the fresher the better, is first choice, but if it's not available, use drained, canned corn instead.

Heat the oil in a large skillet or preheated wok. Add the pork and stir-fry quickly over high heat until lightly browned.

Stir in the garlic, corn, beans, scallions, and chile and continue stir-frying over high heat for 2–3 minutes, until the vegetables are heated through and almost tender.

Stir in the sugar and soy sauce and stir-fry for an additional 30 seconds over high heat.

Sprinkle with the cilantro and serve at once with freshly cooked egg noodles or rice.

cook's tip

In Thailand, yard-long beans would be used for dishes such as this, but you can substitute green beans, which are more easily available. Look out for yard-long beans in Asian grocery stores and markets —they are like long string beans and have a similar flavor, but their texture is crisp, and they cook more quickly.

spicy cooked

ground pork

serves 4

5 minutes

15 minutes

2 garlic cloves
3 shallots
1-inch/2.5-cm piece fresh gingerroot
2 tbsp corn oil
1 lb 2 oz/500 g lean ground pork
2 tbsp Thai fish sauce
1 tbsp dark soy sauce
1 tbsp Thai red curry paste
4 dried kaffir lime leaves, crumbled

4 plum tomatoes, chopped
3 tbsp chopped fresh cilantro
salt and pepper
freshly cooked fine egg noodles,
   to serve

to garnish
fresh cilantro sprigs
scallion tassels

A warmly spiced dish, this is ideal for a quick family meal. Just cook fine egg noodles for an accompaniment while the meat sizzles, and dinner can be on the table in minutes!

Finely chop the garlic, shallots, and ginger. Heat the oil in a large skillet or preheated wok over medium heat. Add the garlic, shallots, and ginger and stir-fry for 2 minutes. Stir in the pork and continue stir-frying until golden brown.

Stir in the fish sauce, soy sauce, curry paste, and lime leaves, and stir-fry for an additional 1–2 minutes over high heat.

Add the chopped tomatoes and cook for an additional 5–6 minutes, stirring occasionally. Stir in the chopped cilantro and season to taste with salt and pepper.

Serve hot, spooned onto freshly cooked fine egg noodles, garnished with cilantro sprigs and scallion tassels.

cook's tip

Dried kaffir lime leaves are a useful pantry ingredient because they can be crumbled straight into quick dishes such as this one. If you prefer to use fresh kaffir lime leaves, shred them finely and add to the dish.

thai-spiced sausages

serves 4

15 minutes

8–10 minutes

¾ cup lean ground pork
1¾ oz/50 g cooked rice
1 garlic clove, crushed
1 tsp Thai red curry paste
1 tsp pepper
1 tsp ground coriander
½ tsp salt
3 tbsp lime juice

2 tbsp chopped fresh cilantro
3 tbsp peanut oil
Chile & Coconut Sambal (see page
   162) or soy sauce, to serve

to garnish

cucumber slices
fresh red chile strips

These mildly spiced little sausages are a good choice for a buffet meal. They can be made a day in advance, and are equally good served hot or cold.

cook's tip

These sausages can also be served as an appetizer— shape the mixture slightly smaller to make 16 bite-size sausages. Serve with a soy dipping sauce.

Place the pork, rice, garlic, curry paste, pepper, ground coriander, salt, lime juice, and chopped cilantro in a bowl and knead together with your hands to mix evenly.

Use your hands to form the mixture into 12 small sausage shapes. If you can buy sausage casings, fill the casings and twist at intervals to separate the sausages.

Heat the oil in a large skillet over medium heat. Add the sausages, in batches if necessary, and cook for 8–10 minutes, turning them over occasionally, until they are evenly golden brown and cooked through. Transfer to a serving plate, garnish with cucumber slices and a few strips of red chile, and serve hot with Chile & Coconut Sambal (see page 162) or soy sauce.

thai-style burgers

serves 4

15 minutes

6–8 minutes

1 small lemon grass stalk
1 small fresh red chile, seeded
2 garlic cloves
2 scallions
7 oz/200 g closed-cup mushrooms
1¾ cups lean ground pork
1 tbsp Thai fish sauce
3 tbsp chopped fresh cilantro
salt and pepper
all-purpose flour, for dusting

corn oil, for pan-frying
2 tbsp mayonnaise
1 tbsp lime juice

to serve

4 sesame hamburger buns
shredded napa cabbage

If your family likes to eat burgers, try these—they have a much more interesting flavor than conventional hamburgers!

cook's tip

You can add a spoonful of your favorite relish to each burger, or alternatively, add a few pieces of Crisp Pickled Vegetables (see page 160) for a change of texture.

Place the lemon grass, chile, garlic, and scallions in a food processor and process to a smooth paste. Add the mushrooms and process until very finely chopped.

Add the pork, fish sauce, and cilantro. Season well with salt and pepper, then divide the mixture into 4 equal portions and form with lightly floured hands into flat burger shapes.

Heat the oil in a skillet over medium heat. Add the burgers and cook for 6–8 minutes, until done or as you like.

Meanwhile, mix the mayonnaise with the lime juice in a small bowl. Split the hamburger buns and spread the lime-flavored mayonnaise on the cut surfaces. Add some shredded napa cabbage, top with a cooked burger, and sandwich together. Serve at once while still hot.

red lamb curry

serves 4

5 minutes

35–40 minutes

1 lb 2 oz/500 g lean, boneless
  leg of lamb
2 tbsp vegetable oil
1 large onion, sliced
2 garlic cloves, crushed
2 tbsp Thai red curry paste
2/3 cup coconut milk
1 tbsp light brown sugar
1 large red bell pepper, seeded and
  thickly sliced

1/2 cup lamb or beef stock
1 tbsp Thai fish sauce
2 tbsp lime juice
8 oz/225 g canned water chestnuts,
  drained
2 tbsp chopped fresh cilantro
2 tbsp chopped fresh basil
salt and pepper
freshly cooked jasmine rice, to serve
fresh basil leaves, to garnish

This richly spiced curry uses the typically red-hot chili flavor of Thai red curry paste, made with dried red chiles, to give it a warm, russet-red color.

variation

This curry can also be made with other lean red meats. Try replacing the lamb with trimmed duck breasts or pieces of lean braising beef.

Trim the meat and cut it into 1½-inch/3-cm cubes. Heat the oil in a large skillet or preheated wok over high heat. Add the onion and garlic and stir-fry for 2–3 minutes to soften. Add the meat and stir-fry the mixture quickly until lightly browned.

Stir in the curry paste and cook for a few seconds, then add the coconut milk and sugar and bring to a boil. Lower the heat and let simmer for 15 minutes, stirring occasionally.

Stir in the red bell pepper, stock, fish sauce, and lime juice, cover and continue simmering for an additional 15 minutes, or until the meat is tender.

Add the water chestnuts, cilantro, and basil and season to taste with salt and pepper. Serve with jasmine rice garnished with basil leaves.

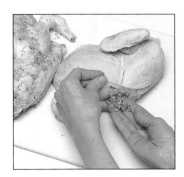

roast chicken with
ginger & lime

serves 4

15 minutes,
plus 8 hours marinating

1 hour 15 minutes

1¼-inch/3-cm piece fresh gingerroot,
   finely chopped
2 garlic cloves, finely chopped
1 small onion, finely chopped
1 lemon grass stalk, finely chopped
½ tsp salt
1 tsp black peppercorns
3 lb 5 oz/1.5 kg roasting chicken

1 tbsp coconut cream
2 tbsp lime juice
2 tbsp honey
1 tsp cornstarch
2 tsp water
freshly cooked stir-fried vegetables,
   to serve

This is a version of a sweet-and-sour chicken dish often sold by street traders in the East—they barbecue the chickens whole or cut in half, then chop them into pieces to sell. Start the preparation the day before you cook, or at least early in the day, to give the flavors plenty of time to penetrate the chicken.

Place the ginger, garlic, onion, lemon grass, salt, and peppercorns in a mortar and, using a pestle, crush to a smooth paste.

Using poultry shears or strong kitchen scissors, cut the chicken in half lengthwise. Spread the paste all over the chicken, both inside and out, and spread it on to the flesh under the breast skin. Cover and let chill in the refrigerator for several hours or overnight.

Preheat the oven to 350°F/180°C. Heat the coconut cream, lime juice, and honey together in a small pan, stirring until smooth. Brush a little of the mixture evenly over the chicken.

Place the chicken halves on a tray over a roasting pan half-filled with boiling water. Roast in the preheated oven for 1 hour, or until the chicken is a rich golden brown, basting occasionally with the lime and honey mixture.

When the chicken is cooked, boil the water from the roasting pan to reduce it to a generous ⅓ cup. Blend the cornstarch and water together and stir into the reduced liquid. Bring gently to a boil, then stir until slightly thickened and clear. Serve the chicken with the sauce and freshly cooked stir-fried vegetables.

chicken &

mango stir-fry

serves 4

5 minutes

12 minutes

6 skinless, boneless chicken thighs
1-inch/2.5-cm piece fresh gingerroot, grated
1 garlic clove, crushed
1 small fresh red chile, seeded and chopped
1 large red bell pepper, seeded
4 scallions
7 oz/200 g snow peas

3½ oz/100 g baby corn
1 large, firm, ripe mango
2 tbsp corn oil
1 tbsp light soy sauce
3 tbsp rice wine or dry sherry
1 tsp sesame oil
salt and pepper
snipped fresh chives, to garnish

A colorful, exotic mix of flavors that works surprisingly well. This dish is easy and quick to cook —ideal for a midweek family meal.

Cut the chicken into long, thin strips and place in a bowl. Mix the ginger, garlic, and chile together in a separate bowl, then stir into the chicken strips to coat them evenly.

Slice the bell pepper thinly, cutting diagonally. Diagonally slice the scallions. Cut the snow peas and baby corn in half diagonally. Peel the mango, remove the seed, and slice thinly.

Heat the oil in a large skillet or preheated wok over high heat. Add the chicken and stir-fry for 4–5 minutes, until just turning golden brown. Add the bell peppers and stir-fry over medium heat for 4–5 minutes, until soft.

Add the scallions, snow peas, and baby corn and stir-fry for an additional 1 minute.

Mix the soy sauce, rice wine, and sesame oil together in a small bowl and stir it into the skillet. Add the mango and stir gently for 1 minute to heat thoroughly.

Season to taste with salt and pepper and serve at once garnished with snipped chives.

thai-spiced
cilantro chicken

serves 4

1 hour 15 minutes

15–20 minutes

4 skinless, boneless chicken breasts
2 garlic cloves
1 fresh green chile, seeded
¾-inch/2-cm piece fresh gingerroot
4 tbsp chopped fresh cilantro
finely grated rind of 1 lime
3 tbsp lime juice
2 tbsp light soy sauce
1 tbsp superfine sugar

¾ cup coconut milk
freshly cooked rice, to serve

to garnish

finely chopped fresh cilantro
cucumber slices
radish slices
½ fresh red chile, seeded and sliced
    into rings

These simple marinated chicken breasts are packed with powerful, zesty flavors and are best accompanied by a simple dish of plain rice and a cucumber salad.

Using a sharp knife, cut 3 deep slashes into the skinned side of each chicken breast. Place the breasts in a single layer in a nonmetallic dish.

Place the garlic, chile, ginger, cilantro, lime rind and juice, soy sauce, sugar, and coconut milk in a food processor and process to a smooth purée.

Spread the purée over both sides of the chicken breasts, coating them evenly. Cover the dish and let marinate in the refrigerator for 1 hour.

Preheat the broiler to medium. Lift the chicken from the marinade, drain off the excess, and place in a broiler pan. Cook under the hot broiler for 12–15 minutes, until thoroughly and evenly cooked.

Meanwhile, place the remaining marinade in a pan and bring to a boil. Lower the heat and let simmer for several minutes to heat thoroughly. Serve with the chicken breasts, accompanied with rice, garnished with chopped cilantro, cucumber slices, radish slices, and chile rings.

green chicken curry

serves 4

10 minutes

50 minutes

6 skinless, boneless chicken thighs
1¾ cups coconut milk
2 garlic cloves, crushed
2 tbsp Thai fish sauce
2 tbsp Thai green curry paste
12 baby eggplants
3 fresh green chiles, finely chopped

3 fresh kaffir lime leaves, shredded,
    plus extra to garnish (optional)
salt and pepper
4 tbsp chopped fresh cilantro
freshly cooked rice, to serve

Thai curries are traditionally very hot, and designed to make a little go a long way—the thin, highly spiced juices are eaten with lots of rice to "stretch" a small amount of meat as far as possible.

cook's tip

Baby eggplants, or "Thai eggplants" as they are called in Thailand, are traditionally used in this curry, but they are not always available. If you can't find them in an Asian store, use chopped ordinary eggplant, or substitute a few green peas.

Cut the chicken into bite-size pieces. Pour the coconut milk into a preheated wok or large skillet over high heat and bring to a boil.

Add the chicken, garlic, and fish sauce to the wok and return to a boil. Lower the heat and let simmer gently for 30 minutes, or until the chicken is just tender.

Remove the chicken from the wok with a slotted spoon. Keep warm.

Stir the curry paste into the wok, add the eggplants, chiles, and lime leaves and let simmer for 5 minutes.

Return the chicken to the wok and bring to a boil. Season to taste with salt and pepper, then stir in the cilantro. Transfer to serving plates, garnish with lime leaves, if using, and serve with freshly cooked rice.

braised chicken with
garlic & spices

serves 4

15 minutes

1 hour

4 garlic cloves, chopped
4 shallots, chopped
2 small fresh red chiles, seeded
  and chopped
1 lemon grass stalk, finely chopped
1 tbsp chopped fresh cilantro
1 tsp shrimp paste
1/2 tsp ground cinnamon
1 tbsp tamarind paste
2 tbsp vegetable oil

8 small chicken joints, such as
  drumsticks or thighs
1 1/4 cups chicken stock
1 tbsp Thai fish sauce
1 tbsp smooth peanut butter
salt and pepper
4 tbsp toasted peanuts, chopped

to serve

stir-fried vegetables
freshly cooked noodles

The intense flavors of this dish are helped by the slow, gentle cooking. The meat should be almost falling off the bone, virtually "melting" into the velvety smooth, spicy sauce.

Place the garlic, shallots, chiles, lemon grass, cilantro, and shrimp paste in a mortar and using a pestle grind to an almost smooth paste. Add the cinnamon and tamarind paste to the mixture.

Heat the oil in a wide skillet or preheated wok. Add the chicken joints, turning frequently, until golden brown on all sides. Remove the chicken from the skillet and keep hot. Tip away any excess fat.

Add the spice paste to the skillet and stir over medium heat until lightly browned. Stir in the stock and return the chicken to the skillet.

Bring to a boil, then cover tightly, lower the heat, and let simmer for 25–30 minutes, stirring occasionally, until the chicken is tender and thoroughly cooked. Stir in the fish sauce and peanut butter and let the mixture simmer for an additional 10 minutes.

Season to taste with salt and pepper and sprinkle the toasted peanuts over the chicken. Serve hot with stir-fried vegetables and noodles.

duck breasts

with chile & lime

serves 4

15 minutes,
plus 3 hours marinating

10 minutes

4 boneless duck breasts
2 garlic cloves, crushed
4 tsp light brown sugar
3 tbsp lime juice
1 tbsp soy sauce
1 tsp chili sauce
1 tsp vegetable oil
2 tbsp plum jelly
1/2 cup chicken stock
salt and pepper

to serve

freshly cooked rice
crisp salad greens

Duck is excellent cooked with strong flavors, and when it is marinated and coated in this rich, dark, sticky Asian glaze it's irresistible. Serve with jasmine rice and a salad.

cook's tip

If you prefer to reduce the overall fat content of this dish, remove the skin from the duck breasts before cooking and reduce the cooking time slightly.

Using a small, sharp knife, cut deep slashes in the skin of the duck to make a diamond pattern. Place the duck breasts in a wide, nonmetallic dish.

Mix the garlic, sugar, lime juice, soy, and chili sauces together in a bowl, then spoon over the duck breasts, turning well to coat evenly. Cover and let marinate in the refrigerator for at least 3 hours or overnight.

Drain the duck, reserving the marinade. Heat a large, heavy-bottom skillet until very hot and brush with the oil. Add the duck breasts, skin-side down, and cook for 5 minutes, or until the skin is browned and crisp. Tip away the excess fat. Turn the duck breasts over.

Continue cooking on the other side for 2–3 minutes to brown. Add the reserved marinade, plum jelly, and stock and let simmer for 2 minutes. Season to taste with salt and pepper. Transfer to serving plates, spoon over the pan juices, and serve hot with freshly cooked rice and salad greens.

roasted duck curried with
pineapple & coconut

 serves 4

 40 minutes

 40 minutes

3 lb 8 oz/1.6 kg duckling
salt and pepper
2 tbsp peanut oil
1 small pineapple
1 large onion, chopped
1 garlic clove, finely chopped
1 tsp finely chopped fresh gingerroot
½ tsp ground coriander

1 tbsp Thai green curry paste
1 tsp light brown sugar
2 cups coconut milk
fresh cilantro, chopped
fresh red and green chile flowers,
    to garnish
freshly cooked jasmine rice, to serve

Duck is a fatty meat, but it has lots of rich flavor. In this recipe, the duckling is "roasted" under a hot broiler until golden brown and crispy, so much of the fat drains off before the meat is added to the curry.

Preheat the broiler to medium. Using a large knife or poultry shears, cut the duckling in half lengthwise, cutting through the line of the breastbone. Wipe inside and out with paper towels. Sprinkle with salt and pepper, prick the skin with a fork, and brush with oil.

Place the duckling, cut-side down, on a broiler pan and cook under the hot broiler for 25–30 minutes, turning occasionally, until golden brown. Tip away the fat in the broiler pan, as it may burn.

Let the duck cool, then cut each half into 2 portions. Peel and core the pineapple, then cut the flesh into dice.

Heat the remaining oil in a large skillet. Add the onion and garlic and cook for 3–4 minutes, until softened. Stir in the ginger, ground coriander, curry paste, and brown sugar and stir-fry for 1 minute.

Stir in the coconut milk and bring to a boil. Add the duckling portions and the pineapple. Lower the heat and let simmer for 5 minutes. Sprinkle with cilantro, garnish with red and green chile flowers, and serve over freshly cooked jasmine rice.

steamed
yellow fish fillets

serves 4

15 minutes

12–15 minutes

1 lb 2 oz/500 g firm fish fillets, such
   as red snapper, sole, or angler fish
1 dried red bird chile
1 small onion, chopped
3 garlic cloves, chopped
2 fresh cilantro sprigs
1 tsp coriander seeds
1/2 tsp ground turmeric

1/2 tsp pepper
1 tbsp Thai fish sauce
2 tbsp coconut milk
1 small egg, beaten
2 tbsp rice flour
fresh red and green chile strips,
   to garnish
stir-fried vegetables, to serve

*Thailand has an abundance of fresh
fish, which is an important part of
the local diet. Dishes such as these
steamed fillets are popular and can
be adapted to suit many different
types of fish. Serve with soy sauce
and a vegetable and bean sprout
salad, if you like.*

cook's tip

*If you don't have a steamer,
improvise by placing a large metal
strainer over a large pan
of boiling water and cover with
an upturned plate to enclose the
fish as it steams.*

Using a sharp knife, remove any skin from the fish and cut the fillets
diagonally into long 3/4-inch/2-cm wide strips.

Place the dried chile, onion, garlic, cilantro, and coriander seeds in a mortar
and, using a pestle, grind to a smooth paste.

Transfer the paste to a bowl and add the turmeric, pepper, fish sauce,
coconut milk, and beaten egg, stirring to mix evenly.

Spread the rice flour out on a large plate. Dip the fish strips into the paste
mixture, then into the rice flour to coat lightly.

Bring the water in the bottom of a steamer to a boil, then arrange the fish
strips in the top of the steamer. Cover and let steam for 12–15 minutes, or
until the fish is just firm.

Garnish with the chile strips and serve at once with stir-fried vegetables.

baked fish with chiles, bell pepper & basil

serves 4

15 minutes

35 minutes

handful of fresh sweet basil leaves
1 lb 10 oz/750 g whole red snapper, sea bass, or porgy, cleaned
2 tbsp peanut oil
2 tbsp Thai fish sauce
2 garlic cloves, crushed
1 tsp finely grated fresh galangal or gingerroot
2 large fresh red chiles, sliced diagonally

1 yellow bell pepper, seeded and diced
1 tbsp jaggery
1 tbsp rice vinegar or white wine vinegar
2 tbsp water or fish stock
2 tomatoes, seeded and sliced into thin wedges
mixed salad, to serve

Almost any whole fish can be cooked by this method, but snapper, sea bass, or porgy are particularly good with the Thai flavors.

cook's tip

Large fresh red chiles are less hot than the tiny red Thai chiles, so you can use them more freely in cooked dishes for a mild heat. Remove the seeds, if you prefer.

Preheat the oven to 375°F/190°C. Set aside a few fresh basil leaves for the garnish and tuck the rest inside the body cavity of the fish.

Heat 1 tablespoon oil in a wide skillet. Add the fish and cook quickly to brown, turning once. Place the fish on a large piece of foil in a roasting pan and spoon over the fish sauce. Wrap the foil over the fish loosely and bake in the preheated oven for 25–30 minutes, or until just cooked through.

Meanwhile, heat the remaining oil in a clean skillet. Add the garlic, galangal, and chiles and cook for 30 seconds. Add the bell pepper and stir-fry for an additional 2–3 minutes to soften.

Stir in the sugar, rice vinegar, and water, then add the tomatoes and bring to a boil. Remove the skillet from the heat.

Remove the fish from the oven and transfer to a warmed serving plate. Add the fish juices to the skillet, then spoon the sauce over the fish. Sprinkle with the reserved basil leaves and serve at once with a salad.

baked cod with a

curry crust

 serves 4

 15 minutes

 35–40 minutes

½ tsp sesame oil
4 cod fillet pieces, about
    5½ oz/150 g each
1½ cups fresh white bread crumbs
2 tbsp blanched almonds, chopped
2 tsp Thai green curry paste
finely grated rind of ½ lime, plus
    extra to garnish
salt and pepper
lime slices, to garnish

to serve

boiled new potatoes
mixed salad greens

An easy, economical main dish that transforms a plain piece of fish into an exotic meal—try it with other white fish, too, such as angler fish or halibut. Serve this with new potatoes and salad.

cook's tip

To test whether the fish is cooked through, use a fork to pierce it in the thickest part—if the flesh is white all the way through and flakes apart easily, it is cooked sufficiently.

Preheat the oven to 400°F/200°C. Brush the sesame oil over the bottom of a wide, shallow ovenproof dish or pan, then arrange the pieces of cod in a single layer.

Mix the bread crumbs, almonds, curry paste, and grated lime rind together in a bowl, stirring well to blend thoroughly and evenly. Season to taste with salt and pepper.

Carefully spoon the crumb mixture over the fish pieces, pressing lightly with your hand to hold it in place.

Bake the dish, uncovered, in the preheated oven for 35–40 minutes, or until the fish is cooked through and the crumb topping is golden brown.

Serve the dish hot, garnished with lime slices and rind and accompanied by boiled new potatoes and mixed salad greens.

whole fried fish with soy & ginger

serves 4–6

20 minutes

20 minutes

6 dried Chinese mushrooms
3 tbsp rice vinegar
2 tbsp light brown sugar
3 tbsp dark soy sauce
3-inch/7.5-cm piece fresh gingerroot,
   finely chopped
4 scallions, sliced diagonally
2 tsp cornstarch
2 tbsp lime juice

1 sea bass, about 2 lb 4 oz/1 kg,
   cleaned
salt and pepper
4 tbsp all-purpose flour
corn oil, for cooking
1 radish, sliced but left whole,
   to garnish

to serve

shredded napa cabbage
radish slices

This impressive dish is worth cooking for a special dinner, as it really is a talking point. Buy a very fresh whole fish on the day you plan to cook it, and ask the store to clean it, preferably leaving the head on.

Place the dried mushrooms in a bowl, cover with hot water, and let soak for 10 minutes. Drain well, reserving generous ⅓ cup of the liquid. Cut the mushrooms into thin slices.

Mix the reserved mushroom liquid with the rice vinegar, sugar, and soy sauce. Place in a pan with the mushrooms and bring to a boil. Lower the heat and let simmer for 3–4 minutes.

Add the ginger and scallions and let simmer for 1 minute. Blend the cornstarch and lime juice together, stir into the pan, and stir for 1–2 minutes, until the sauce thickens and clears. Set aside until required.

Season the fish inside and out with salt and pepper, then dust lightly with flour, carefully shaking off the excess.

Heat a 1-inch/2.5-cm depth of oil in a wide skillet to 375°F/190°C, or until a cube of bread browns in 30 seconds. Carefully lower the fish into the oil and cook on one side for 3–4 minutes, until golden. Use 2 metal spatulas to turn the fish carefully and cook on the other side for an additional 3–4 minutes, until golden brown.

Lift the fish out of the skillet, draining off the excess oil and place on a serving plate. Heat the reserved sauce until boiling, then spoon it over the fish. Serve at once, surrounded by shredded napa cabbage with sliced radishes, and garnished with the sliced whole radish.

spiced tuna in
sweet & sour sauce

serves 4

10 minutes

15 minutes

4 fresh tuna steaks, about
  1 lb 2 oz/500 g total weight
¼ tsp pepper
2 tbsp peanut oil
1 onion, diced
1 small red bell pepper, seeded and
  cut into short thin sticks
1 garlic clove, crushed
½ cucumber, seeded and cut into
  short thin sticks
2 pineapple slices, diced

1 tsp finely chopped fresh gingerroot
1 tbsp light brown sugar
1 tbsp cornstarch
1½ tbsp lime juice
1 tbsp Thai fish sauce
generous 1 cup fish stock

to garnish

lime slices
cucumber slices

Tuna is a firm, meaty textured fish that is abundant in the seas round Thailand. You can also use shark or mackerel with this rich sweet-and-sour sauce.

cook's tip

Tuna can be served quite lightly cooked. It can be dry if overcooked.

Sprinkle the tuna steaks with pepper on both sides. Heat a heavy-bottom skillet or ridged griddle and brush with a little of the oil. Arrange the tuna in the skillet and cook for 8 minutes, turning them over once.

Meanwhile, heat the remaining oil in a separate skillet. Add the onion, bell pepper, and garlic and cook gently for 3–4 minutes to soften.

Remove the skillet from the heat and stir in the cucumber, pineapple, ginger, and sugar.

Blend the cornstarch with the lime juice and fish sauce, then stir into the stock and add to the skillet. Stir over medium heat until boiling, then cook for 1–2 minutes, until thickened and clear.

Spoon the sauce over the tuna and serve at once garnished with lime slices and cucumber.

thai-spiced salmon

serves 4

40 minutes

4–5 minutes

1-inch/2.5-cm piece fresh gingerroot, grated
1 tsp coriander seeds, crushed
1/4 tsp chili powder
1 tbsp lime juice
1 tsp sesame oil
4 salmon fillet pieces with skin, about 5 1/2 oz/150 g each
2 tbsp vegetable oil
fresh cilantro leaves, to garnish

to serve
freshly cooked rice
stir-fried vegetables

Marinated in delicate Thai spices and quickly pan-fried to perfection, these salmon fillets are ideal for a special dinner. Serve them fresh from the skillet to enjoy them at their best.

cook's tip

It's important to use a heavy-bottom skillet or solid griddle for this recipe to ensure that the fish cooks evenly throughout without sticking. If the fish is very thick, you may prefer to turn it over to cook on the other side for 2–3 minutes.

Mix the ginger, crushed coriander, chili powder, lime juice, and sesame oil together in a bowl.

Place the salmon on a wide, nonmetallic plate or dish and spoon the mixture over the flesh side of the fillets, spreading it to coat each piece of salmon evenly.

Cover the dish with plastic wrap and let chill in the refrigerator for 30 minutes.

Heat a wide, heavy-bottom skillet or ridged griddle with the vegetable oil over high heat. Place the salmon in the hot skillet, skin-side down, and cook for 4–5 minutes, without turning, until the salmon is crusty underneath and the flesh flakes easily.

Serve at once with freshly cooked rice, garnished with cilantro leaves, and stir-fried vegetables.

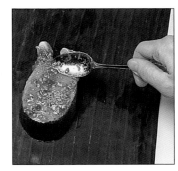

salmon with red curry in banana leaves

serves 4

10 minutes

15–20 minutes

4 salmon steaks, about
  6 oz/175 g each
2 banana leaves, halved
1 garlic clove, crushed
1 tsp grated fresh gingerroot
1 tbsp Thai red curry paste
1 tsp light brown sugar
1 tbsp Thai fish sauce
2 tbsp lime juice

to garnish

lime wedges
whole fresh red chiles
finely chopped fresh red chile

Banana leaves are widely used in Thai cooking to wrap raw ingredients such as fish before baking or steaming. Asian grocery stores and markets usually stock them, but if you can't find any use foil or parchment paper instead.

cook's tip

Fresh banana leaves are often sold in packages containing several leaves, but if you buy more than you need, they will store in the refrigerator for about 1 week.

Preheat the oven to 425°F/220°C. Place a salmon steak on the center of each half banana leaf.

Mix the garlic, ginger, curry paste, sugar, and fish sauce together, then spread over the surface of the fish and sprinkle with lime juice.

Wrap the banana leaves round the fish, tucking in the sides as you go to make a neat, compact bundle.

Place the packages seam-side down on a baking sheet and bake in the preheated oven for 15–20 minutes, or until the fish is cooked and the banana leaves are starting to brown. Serve garnished with lime wedges, whole chiles, and finely chopped chile.

spicy thai
seafood stew

serves 4

5 minutes

10 minutes

7 oz/200 g squid, cleaned and
  tentacles discarded
1 lb 2 oz/500 g firm white fish fillet,
  preferably angler fish or halibut
1 tbsp corn oil
4 shallots, finely chopped
2 garlic cloves, finely chopped
2 tbsp Thai green curry paste
2 small lemon grass stalks, finely
  chopped

1 tsp shrimp paste
generous 2 cups coconut milk
7 oz/200 g raw jumbo shrimp, shelled
  and deveined
12 fresh clams in shells, cleaned
8 basil leaves, finely shredded
fresh basil leaves, to garnish
freshly cooked rice, to serve

*The fish in this fragrant, currylike
stew can be varied according to
taste or availability, but it's best
to stick with those which stay firm
when cooked because delicate types
will flake apart too easily.*

variation

*If you prefer, live mussels in shells
can be used instead of clams—add
them after the shrimp and continue
as in the recipe.*

Using a sharp knife, cut the squid body cavities into thick rings and the fish
into bite-size chunks.

Heat the oil in a large skillet or preheated wok. Add the shallots, garlic, and
curry paste and stir-fry for 1–2 minutes. Add the lemon grass and shrimp
paste, stir in the coconut milk and bring to a boil.

Lower the heat until the liquid is simmering gently, then add the white fish,
squid, and shrimp to the skillet and let simmer for 2 minutes.

Add the clams and let simmer for an additional 1 minute, until the clams
open. Discard any clams that remain closed.

Sprinkle the shredded basil leaves over the stew. Transfer to serving plates,
garnish with whole basil leaves, and serve at once with rice.

stir-fried squid with hot black bean sauce

serves 4

15 minutes

5–10 minutes

1 lb 10 oz/750 g squid, cleaned and
   tentacles discarded
1 large red bell pepper, seeded
3 oz/85 g snow peas
1 head bok choy
3 tbsp black bean sauce
1 tbsp Thai fish sauce
1 tbsp rice wine or dry sherry
1 tbsp dark soy sauce
1 tsp light brown sugar

1 tsp cornstarch
1 tbsp water
1 tbsp corn oil
1 tsp sesame oil
1 small fresh red Thai chile, chopped
1 garlic clove, finely chopped
1 tsp grated fresh gingerroot
2 scallions, chopped

Quick stir-frying is an ideal cooking method for squid, because if overcooked it can be tough. The technique also seals in the natural colors, flavors, and nutritional value of fresh vegetables.

Cut the squid body cavities into quarters lengthwise. Use the tip of a small sharp knife to score a diamond pattern into the flesh, without cutting all the way through. Pat dry with paper towels.

Cut the bell pepper into long, thin slices. Cut the snow peas in half diagonally. Coarsely shred the bok choy.

Mix the black bean sauce, fish sauce, rice wine, soy sauce, and sugar together in a bowl. Blend the cornstarch with the water and stir into the other sauce ingredients. Set aside until required.

Heat the oils in a preheated wok. Add the chile, garlic, ginger, and scallions and stir-fry for 1 minute. Add the bell pepper and stir-fry for 2 minutes.

Add the squid and stir-fry over high heat for an additional 1 minute. Stir in the snow peas and bok choy and stir for an additional 1 minute, until wilted.

Stir in the sauce ingredients and cook, stirring constantly, for 2 minutes, until the sauce thickens and clears. Serve at once.

spicy scallops
with lime & chile

serves 4

10 minutes

8 minutes

16 large scallops
1 tbsp butter
1 tbsp vegetable oil
1 tsp crushed garlic
1 tsp grated fresh gingerroot
1 bunch of scallions, finely sliced
finely grated rind of 1 lime

1 small fresh red chile, seeded and
   very finely chopped
3 tbsp lime juice
lime wedges, to garnish
freshly cooked rice, to serve

Really fresh scallops have a delicate flavor and texture, needing only a minimal amount of cooking, as in this simple stir-fry.

cook's tip

If fresh scallops are not available, frozen ones can be used, but make sure they are thoroughly thawed before you cook them. Drain off all excess moisture and pat dry with paper towels.

Using a sharp knife, trim the scallops to remove any black intestine, then wash and pat dry with paper towels. Separate the corals from the white parts, then horizontally slice each white part in half, making 2 circles.

Heat the butter and oil in a skillet or preheated wok. Add the garlic and ginger and stir-fry for 1 minute without browning. Add the scallions and stir-fry for an additional 1 minute.

Add the scallops and continue stir-frying over high heat for 4–5 minutes. Stir in the lime rind, chile, and lime juice and cook for an additional 1 minute.

Transfer the scallops to serving plates, spoon over the pan juices, and garnish with lime wedges. Serve hot with freshly cooked rice.

shrimp skewers with
chile & tamarind glaze

serves 4

2 hours 15 minutes

10 minutes

1 garlic clove, chopped
1 fresh red Thai chile, seeded and
  chopped
1 tbsp tamarind paste
1 tbsp sesame oil
1 tbsp dark soy sauce
2 tbsp lime juice
1 tbsp soft light brown sugar
16 large whole raw jumbo shrimp
lime wedges, to garnish

to serve

crusty bread
salad greens

Whole jumbo shrimp cook very quickly on a barbecue or under a broiler, so they are ideal for summertime cooking, indoors or outside. All you need is a fresh salad and the meal is complete. Hand round rose-scented finger bowls so guests can easily clean their hands.

Place the garlic, chile, tamarind, sesame oil, soy sauce, lime juice, and sugar in a small pan. Stir over low heat until the sugar is dissolved, then remove the pan from the heat and let cool completely.

Wash the shrimp under cold running water and pat dry with paper towels. Arrange in a single layer in a wide, nonmetallic dish. Spoon the marinade over the shrimp and turn to coat evenly. Cover and let marinate in the refrigerator for at least 2 hours or preferably overnight.

Meanwhile, soak 4 bamboo or wooden skewers in water for 20 minutes. Preheat the broiler to medium.

Thread 4 shrimp onto each presoaked skewer and cook under the hot broiler for 5–6 minutes, turning them over once, until they turn pink and start to brown. Alternatively, barbecue over hot coals.

Thread a wedge of lime onto the end of each skewer and serve with crusty bread and salad greens.

rice & noodles

With its monsoon climate and abundant rainfall, Thailand has the ideal conditions for rice growing and has become one of the major rice producers in the world. It is thought that rice grew there as far back as 3500 BCE. So it is not surprising that rice is the staple food in Thailand. Hardly a meal goes by without it appearing in some form or another.

Two main varieties of rice are used in Thai cooking—a long-grain and a short-grain. The long-grain is Thai fragrant rice, a good-quality white, fluffy rice with delicately scented, separate grains. Glutinous or "sticky" rice is a short-grain rice with a high starch content that causes the grains to stick together.

Noodles also play a vital part in Thai meals, and street vendors serve them as a snack at all times of the day. Rice noodles in flat ribbons (sticks) or thin vermicelli are the most common, and these need to be soaked before being cooked or added to soups and stir-fries. Cellophane (mung bean) noodles are also locally made, but egg noodles are often imported from China. Most noodle dishes are served with an array of condiments for the diner to add to his or her taste—usually including crushed dried chiles, finely chopped peanuts, Thai fish sauce, soy sauce, and sugar.

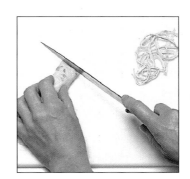

crispy rice noodles

serves 4

5 minutes

15 minutes

vegetable oil, for deep-frying, plus
  1½ tbsp
7 oz/200 g rice vermicelli noodles
1 onion, finely chopped
4 garlic cloves, finely chopped
1 skinless, boneless chicken breast,
  finely chopped
2 fresh red Thai chiles, seeded
  and sliced
4 tbsp dried black mushrooms,
  soaked and thinly sliced
3 tbsp dried shrimp

4 scallions, sliced
3 tbsp lime juice
2 tbsp soy sauce
2 tbsp Thai fish sauce
2 tbsp rice vinegar or white
  wine vinegar
2 tbsp light brown sugar
2 eggs, beaten
3 tbsp chopped fresh cilantro
scallion curls, to garnish

This is a version of a favorite Thai dish, "mee krob," one of those exciting dishes which varies from one household to another and one day to the next—depending on the ingredients available.

Heat the oil in a large skillet or preheated wok until very hot. Add the noodles and deep-fry quickly, occasionally turning them, until puffed up, crisp and pale golden brown. Lift onto paper towels and drain well.

Heat 1 tablespoon oil in a separate skillet. Add the onion and garlic and sauté for 1 minute. Add the chicken and stir-fry for 3 minutes. Add the chiles, mushrooms, dried shrimp, and scallions.

Mix the lime juice, soy sauce, fish sauce, rice vinegar, and sugar together, then stir into the skillet and cook for an additional 1 minute. Remove the skillet from the heat.

Heat the remaining oil in a wide skillet. Pour in the eggs to coat the bottom of the skillet evenly, making a thin omelet. Cook until set and golden, then turn it over and cook the other side. Turn out and roll up, then slice into long ribbon strips.

Toss the cooked noodles, stir-fried ingredients, cilantro, and omelet strips together. Garnish with scallion curls and serve at once.

sesame noodles with
shrimp & cilantro

serves 4

5 minutes

10 minutes

1 garlic clove, chopped
1 scallion, chopped
1 small fresh red chile, seeded
  and sliced
1 handful of fresh cilantro
10½ oz/300 g fine egg noodles
2 tbsp vegetable oil
2 tsp sesame oil

1 tsp shrimp paste
8 oz/225 g raw shrimp, shelled
2 tbsp lime juice
2 tbsp Thai fish sauce
1 tsp sesame seeds, toasted

Delicately scented with sesame and cilantro, these noodles make an unusual lunch or supper dish.

cook's tip

The roots of cilantro are widely used in Thai cooking, so if you can buy fresh cilantro with the root attached, the whole plant can be used in this dish for maximum flavor. If not, just use the stems and leaves.

Place the garlic, onion, chile, and cilantro in a mortar and, using a pestle, grind to a smooth paste.

Drop the noodles into a pan of boiling water and return to a boil, then let simmer for 4 minutes, or according to the package instructions.

Meanwhile, heat the oils in a large skillet or preheated wok. Stir in the shrimp paste and ground cilantro mixture and stir over medium heat for 1 minute.

Stir in the shrimp and stir-fry for 2 minutes. Stir in the lime juice and fish sauce and cook for an additional 1 minute.

Drain the noodles and toss them into the skillet. Sprinkle with the sesame seeds and serve at once.

hot & sour noodles

serves 4

5 minutes

8 minutes

9 oz/250 g dried medium egg noodles
1 tbsp sesame oil
1 tbsp chili oil
1 garlic clove, crushed
2 scallions, finely chopped
2 oz/55 g white mushrooms, sliced
1 1/2 oz/40 g dried Chinese black mushrooms, soaked, drained, and sliced
2 tbsp lime juice

3 tbsp light soy sauce
1 tsp sugar

to serve

shredded napa cabbage
2 tbsp shredded coriander
2 tbsp toasted peanuts, chopped

This simple, fast food dish is sold from street food stalls in Thailand, with many and varied additions of meat and vegetables. It is equally good served hot or cold.

cook's tip

Thai chili oil is very hot, so if you want a milder flavor, use vegetable oil for the initial cooking instead, then add a final dribble of chili oil just for seasoning.

Cook the noodles in a large pan of boiling water for 3–4 minutes, or according to the package instructions. Drain well, return to the pan, toss with the sesame oil, and set aside.

Heat the chili oil in a large skillet or preheated wok. Add the garlic, onions, and white mushrooms and quickly stir-fry to soften them.

Add the black mushrooms, lime juice, soy sauce, and sugar and continue stir-frying until boiling. Add the noodles and toss to mix.

Arrange the noodles on a bed of napa cabbage, sprinkle with cilantro and peanuts, and serve.

pad thai noodles

serves 4

10 minutes

5 minutes

9 oz/250 g rice stick noodles
3 tbsp peanut oil
3 garlic cloves, finely chopped
4¹/₂ oz/125 g pork fillet, chopped into
    ¹/₄-inch/5-mm pieces
7 oz/200 g cooked shelled shrimp
1 tbsp sugar
3 tbsp Thai fish sauce
1 tbsp tomato ketchup

1 tbsp lime juice
2 eggs, beaten
generous ³/₄ cup bean sprouts

to garnish

1 tsp dried red pepper flakes
2 scallions, thickly sliced
2 tbsp chopped fresh cilantro

The combination of ingredients in this classic noodle dish varies, depending on the cook, but it commonly contains a mixture of pork and shrimp or other seafood.

cook's tip

Drain the rice noodles before adding to the wok because excess moisture will spoil the texture of the dish.

Place the rice noodles in a bowl, cover with hot water, and let soak for 15 minutes, or according to the package instructions. Drain well and set aside until required.

Heat the oil in a large skillet. Add the garlic and sauté over high heat for 30 seconds. Add the pork and stir-fry for 2–3 minutes, until browned.

Stir in the shrimp, then add the sugar, fish sauce, tomato ketchup, and lime juice and continue stir-frying for an additional 30 seconds.

Stir in the eggs and stir-fry until lightly set. Stir in the reserved noodles, then add the bean sprouts and stir-fry for an additional 30 seconds.

Transfer to a serving dish and sprinkle with red pepper flakes, scallions, and cilantro. Serve at once.

rice noodles with
mushrooms & tofu

serves 4

20 minutes

8–10 minutes

8 oz/225 g rice stick noodles
2 tbsp vegetable oil
1 garlic clove, finely chopped
3/4-inch/2-cm piece fresh gingerroot, finely chopped
4 shallots, thinly sliced
2 1/2 oz/70 g shiitake mushrooms, sliced
3 1/2 oz/100 g firm tofu, cut into 5/8-inch/1.5-cm dice (drained weight)

2 tbsp light soy sauce
1 tbsp rice wine or dry sherry
1 tbsp Thai fish sauce
1 tbsp smooth peanut butter
1 tsp chili sauce
2 tbsp toasted peanuts, chopped
shredded fresh basil leaves

An alternative to classic dishes such as Pad Thai Noodles (see page 134), this quick and easy dish is very filling. If you omit the fish sauce, it can be served as a vegetarian dish.

variation

For an easy pantry dish, replace the shiitake mushrooms with canned Chinese straw mushrooms. Alternatively, use dried shiitake mushrooms, soaked and drained before use.

Place the rice stick noodles in a bowl, cover with hot water, and let soak for 15 minutes, or according to the package instructions. Drain well.

Heat the oil in a large skillet. Add the garlic, ginger, and shallots and stir-fry for 1–2 minutes, until softened and lightly browned.

Add the mushrooms and stir-fry for an additional 2–3 minutes. Stir in the tofu and toss gently to brown lightly.

Mix the soy sauce, rice wine, fish sauce, peanut butter, and chili sauce together in a small bowl, then stir into the skillet.

Stir in the rice noodles and toss to coat evenly in the sauce. Sprinkle with peanuts and shredded basil leaves and serve hot.

thai-style
noodle rostis

serves 4

5 minutes

10 minutes

4¹/₂ oz/125 g vermicelli rice noodles
2 scallions, finely shredded
1 lemon grass stalk, finely shredded
3 tbsp finely shredded fresh coconut
vegetable oil, for cooking

to serve

³/₄ cup bean sprouts
1 small red onion, thinly sliced
1 avocado, thinly sliced
2 tbsp lime juice
2 tbsp rice wine or dry sherry
1 tsp chili sauce
whole fresh red chiles, to garnish

*Serve these crisp, fried "rösti"
noodle crêpes as an unusual first
course, or as a decorative side dish
alongside meat dishes.*

Break the rice noodles into short pieces and place in a bowl, cover with hot water, and let soak for 4 minutes, or according to the package instructions. Drain thoroughly and pat dry with paper towels.

Stir the noodles, scallions, lemon grass, and coconut together.

Heat a small amount of oil until very hot in a heavy-bottom skillet. Brush a 3¹/₂-inch/9-cm round cookie cutter with oil and place in the skillet. Spoon a small amount of noodle mixture into the cutter to just cover the bottom of the skillet, then press down with the back of a spoon.

Cook for 30 seconds, then carefully remove the cutter and continue cooking the rösti until golden brown, turning it over once. Remove and drain on paper towels. Repeat with the remaining noodles, to make 12 röstis.

To serve, arrange the noodle röstis in small stacks, with bean sprouts, onion, and avocado between the layers. Mix the lime juice, rice wine, and chili sauce together and spoon over just before serving, garnished with whole red chiles.

drunken noodles

serves 4

20 minutes

8–10 minutes

6 oz/175 g rice stick noodles
2 tbsp vegetable oil
1 garlic clove, crushed
2 small fresh green chiles, chopped
1 small onion, thinly sliced
scant ³⁄₄ cup lean cooked ground pork or chicken
1 small green bell pepper, seeded and finely chopped

4 fresh kaffir lime leaves, finely shredded
1 tbsp dark soy sauce
1 tbsp light soy sauce
½ tsp sugar
1 tomato, cut into thin wedges
2 tbsp finely sliced sweet basil leaves

Perhaps this would be more correctly named "drunkards' noodles," as it's a dish that is supposedly often eaten as a hangover cure—the fiery kick of the chiles wakes up the system and the lime leaves and basil cleanse and refresh the palate.

cook's tip

Fresh kaffir lime leaves freeze well, so if you buy more than you need, simply pop them in a tightly sealed plastic freezer bag and freeze for up to 1 month. They can be used straight from the freezer.

Place the rice stick noodles in a bowl, cover with hot water, and let soak for 15 minutes, or according to the package instructions. Drain well.

Heat the oil in a large skillet or preheated wok. Add the garlic, chiles, and onion and stir-fry for 1 minute.

Stir in the pork and stir-fry over high heat for an additional 1 minute, then add the bell pepper and continue stir-frying for an additional 2 minutes.

Stir in the lime leaves, soy sauces, and sugar. Add the noodles and tomato and toss well to heat thoroughly.

Sprinkle with the sliced basil leaves and serve hot.

crispy duck with
noodles & tamarind

serves 4

1 hour 15 minutes

20 minutes

3 duck breasts, total weight about
  14 oz/400 g
2 garlic cloves, crushed
1½ tsp chili paste
1 tbsp honey
3 tbsp dark soy sauce
½ tsp Chinese five-spice powder
9 oz/250 g rice stick noodles

1 tsp vegetable oil
1 tsp sesame oil
2 scallions, sliced
3½ oz/100 g snow peas
2 tbsp tamarind juice
sesame seeds, for sprinkling

A robustly flavored dish that makes a substantial main course. Serve it with a refreshing cucumber salad or a light vegetable stir-fry.

Prick the duck breast skin all over with a fork and place in a deep dish.

Mix the garlic, chili, honey, soy sauce, and five-spice powder together, then pour over the duck. Turn the breasts over to coat evenly, then cover and let marinate in the refrigerator for at least 1 hour.

Meanwhile, place the rice noodles in a bowl, cover with hot water, and let soak for 15 minutes. Drain well.

Preheat the broiler to high. Drain the duck breasts from the marinade and place on a broiler rack. Cook under the hot broiler for 10 minutes, turning them over occasionally, until they are a rich golden brown color. Remove and slice the duck breasts thinly.

Heat the vegetable and sesame oils in a skillet. Add the scallions and snow peas and toss for 2 minutes. Stir in the reserved marinade and tamarind juice and bring to a boil.

Add the sliced duck and noodles and toss to heat thoroughly. Serve at once, sprinkled with sesame seeds.

rice noodles with chicken & napa cabbage

 serves 4

 25 minutes

 10 minutes

7 oz/200 g rice stick noodles
1 tbsp corn oil
1 garlic clove, finely chopped
3/4-inch/2-cm piece fresh gingerroot, finely chopped
4 scallions, chopped
1 fresh red Thai chile, seeded and sliced
10½ oz/300 g skinless, boneless chicken, finely chopped
2 chicken livers, finely chopped

1 celery stalk, thinly sliced
1 carrot, cut into fine thin sticks
10½ oz/300 g shredded napa cabbage
4 tbsp lime juice
2 tbsp Thai fish sauce
1 tbsp soy sauce
2 tbsp shredded fresh mint
slices of pickled garlic
fresh mint sprigs, to garnish

The great thing about stir-fries is you can cook with very little fat and still get lots of flavor. This light, healthy lunch dish is low in fat and very quick to make.

Place the rice noodles in a bowl, cover with hot water, and let soak for 15 minutes, or according to the package instructions. Drain well.

Heat the oil in a large skillet or preheated wok. Add the garlic, ginger, scallions, and chile and stir-fry for 1 minute. Stir in the chicken and chicken livers and stir-fry over high heat for 2–3 minutes, until starting to brown.

Stir in the celery and carrot and stir-fry for 2 minutes to soften. Add the napa cabbage, then stir in the lime juice, fish sauce, and soy sauce.

Add the noodles and stir to heat thoroughly. Sprinkle with shredded mint and pickled garlic. Serve at once, garnished with mint sprigs.

rice noodles
with spinach

serves 4

20 minutes

6–8 minutes

4 oz/115 g thin rice stick noodles
2 tbsp dried shrimp (optional)
5⅝ cups fresh young spinach
1 tbsp peanut oil
2 garlic cloves, finely chopped
2 tsp Thai green curry paste
1 tsp sugar
1 tbsp light soy sauce

This quick stir-fried noodle dish is simple to prepare, and makes a delicious light lunch in minutes. You can leave out the dried shrimp, or replace them with chopped peanuts for a vegetarian dish.

cook's tip

It is best to choose young spinach leaves for this dish because they are beautifully tender and cook within a matter of seconds. If you can only get older spinach, however, shred the leaves before adding to the dish so they cook more quickly.

Place the noodles in a bowl, cover with hot water, and let soak for 15 minutes, or according to the package instructions. Drain well.

Place the shrimp, if using, in a bowl, cover with hot water, and let soak for 10 minutes. Drain well. Wash the spinach thoroughly, drain well, and remove any tough stalks.

Heat the oil in a large skillet or preheated wok. Add the garlic and stir-fry for 1 minute. Stir in the curry paste and stir-fry for 30 seconds. Stir in the soaked shrimp and stir-fry for 30 seconds.

Add the spinach and stir-fry for 1–2 minutes, or until the leaves are just wilted.

Stir in the sugar and soy sauce, then add the noodles and toss thoroughly to mix evenly. Serve at once while hot.

egg noodle salad
with coconut, lime & basil dressing

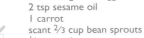

serves 4

20 minutes

4–5 minutes

8 oz/225 g dried egg noodles
2 tsp sesame oil
1 carrot
scant 2/3 cup bean sprouts
1/2 cucumber
2 scallions, finely shredded
5 1/2 oz/150 g cooked turkey breast
    meat, shredded into thin slivers
chopped peanuts, for sprinkling
fresh basil leaves, to garnish

dressing

5 tbsp coconut milk
3 tbsp lime juice
1 tbsp light soy sauce
2 tsp Thai fish sauce
1 tsp chili oil
1 tsp sugar
2 tbsp chopped fresh cilantro
2 tbsp chopped fresh sweet basil

A good dish for summer eating, this is light and refreshing in flavor and easy to cook. The turkey can be replaced with cooked chicken, if you prefer.

Cook the noodles in boiling water for 4 minutes, or according to the package instructions. Plunge them into a bowl of cold water to cool, then drain and toss in sesame oil.

Use a vegetable peeler to shave off thin ribbons from the carrot. Blanch the ribbons and bean sprouts in boiling water for 30 seconds, then plunge into cold water for 30 seconds. Drain well. Next, shave thin ribbons of cucumber with the vegetable peeler.

Toss the carrot, bean sprouts, cucumber, and scallions together with the turkey and noodles.

Place all the dressing ingredients in a screw-top jar and shake well to mix evenly.

Add the dressing to the noodle mixture and toss. Pile onto a serving dish. Sprinkle with peanuts and garnish with basil leaves. Serve cold.

stir-fried rice
with egg strips

serves 4

5–10 minutes

5 minutes

2 tbsp peanut oil
1 egg, beaten with 1 tsp water
1 garlic clove, finely chopped
1 small onion, finely chopped
1 tbsp Thai red curry paste
generous 3⅜ cups long-grain rice, cooked
½ cup cooked peas

1 tbsp Thai fish sauce
2 tbsp tomato ketchup
2 tbsp chopped fresh cilantro

to garnish
fresh red chile flowers
cucumber slices

Many Thai rice dishes are made from leftover rice that has been cooked for an earlier meal. But nothing goes to waste and it's often stir-fried with a few simple ingredients and aromatic flavorings, as in this recipe. If you have any leftover vegetables or meat, this is a good way to use them up.

To make chile flowers for the garnish, hold the stem of a fresh red chile with your fingertips and use a small sharp, pointed knife to cut a slit down the length from near the stem end to the tip. Turn the chile about a quarter turn and make another cut. Repeat to make a total of 4 cuts, then scrape out the seeds. Cut each "petal" again in half, or into quarters, to make 8–16 petals. Place the chile in iced water.

Heat 1 teaspoon of the oil in a preheated wok or large skillet. Pour in the egg mixture, swirling it to coat the wok evenly and make a thin layer. When set and golden, remove the egg from the wok and roll up. Set aside until required.

Add the remaining oil to the wok. Add the garlic and onion and stir-fry for 1 minute. Add the curry paste, then stir in the rice and peas.

Stir in the fish sauce and ketchup. Remove the wok from the heat and pile the rice onto a serving dish.

Slice the egg roll into spiral strips, without unrolling, and use to garnish the rice. Add the cucumber slices and chile flowers. Serve hot.

jasmine rice
with lemon & basil

serves 4

15 minutes

15 minutes

2 cups jasmine rice
generous 3 cups water
finely grated rind of $1/2$ lemon
2 tbsp shredded fresh sweet basil

Jasmine rice has a delicate flavor and it can be served completely plain, with no other flavorings. This simple dish just has the light tang of lemon and soft scent of basil to add an extra touch.

cook's tip

It is important to leave the pan tightly covered while the rice cooks and steams inside, so the grains cook evenly and become fluffy and separate.

Wash the rice in several changes of cold water until the water runs clear. Bring the water to a boil in a large pan, then add the rice.

Return to a rolling boil. Turn the heat to a low simmer, cover the pan, and let simmer for an additional 12 minutes.

Remove the pan from the heat and let stand, covered, for 10 minutes.

Fluff up the rice with a fork, then stir in the lemon rind. Serve sprinkle with shredded basil.

rice with seafood

serves 4

5–10 minutes

20 minutes

12 live mussels in shells, cleaned
generous 8 cups fish stock
2 tbsp vegetable oil
1 garlic clove, crushed
1 tsp grated fresh gingerroot
1 fresh red Thai chile, chopped
2 scallions, chopped
generous 1 cup long-grain rice
2 small squid, cleaned and sliced

3½ oz/100 g firm white fish fillet,
  such as halibut or angler fish, cut
  into chunks
3½ oz/100 g raw shrimp, shelled
2 tbsp Thai fish sauce
3 tbsp shredded fresh cilantro

*This souplike main course rice dish
is packed with fresh seafood,
and typically Thai in flavor. If you
have time, make your own fish
stock from fish trimmings, or use
good-quality bouillon cubes.*

variation

*You could use leftover cooked rice
for this dish. Just simmer the
seafood gently until cooked, then stir
in the rice at the end.*

Discard any mussels with damaged shells or ones that do not close when firmly tapped. Heat 4 tablespoons of the stock in a large pan. Add the mussels, cover, and cook, shaking the pan occasionally, until the mussels open. Remove the pan from the heat and discard any mussels that remain closed.

Heat the oil in a large skillet or preheated wok. Add the garlic, ginger, chile, and scallions and stir-fry for 30 seconds. Add the stock and bring to a boil.

Stir in the rice, then add the squid, fish fillet, and shrimp. Lower the heat and let simmer gently for 15 minutes, or until the rice is cooked. Add the fish sauce and mussels.

Ladle into wide bowls and sprinkle with cilantro before serving.

coconut rice with
pineapple

serves 4

5 minutes

20 minutes

1 cup long-grain rice
generous 2 cups coconut milk
2 lemon grass stalks
scant 1 cup water
2 slices fresh pineapple, peeled
 and diced
2 tbsp toasted coconut
chili sauce, to serve

Cooking rice in coconut milk makes it very satisfying and nutritious, and is often used as a base for main dishes, with the addition of meat, fish, vegetables, or eggs to make it more substantial.

variation

A sweet version of this dish can be made by simply omitting the lemon grass and stirring in jaggery or superfine sugar to taste during cooking. Serve as a dessert, with extra pineapple slices.

Wash the rice in several changes of cold water until the water runs clear. Place in a large pan with the coconut milk.

Place the lemon grass on a counter and bruise it by hitting firmly with a rolling pin or mallet. Add to the pan with the rice and coconut milk.

Add the water and bring to a boil. Lower the heat, cover the pan tightly, and let simmer gently for 15 minutes. Remove the pan from the heat and fluff up the rice with a fork.

Remove the lemon grass and stir in the pineapple. Sprinkle with toasted coconut and serve with chili sauce.

vegetables & salads

Many of the vegetables, salad greens, and shoots that Thais use in vegetable dishes and salads are native, often growing wild locally. This makes it difficult to produce really authentic Thai salads at home, as even the best Asian food stores and markets cannot source all the fresh ingredients.

You may have to replace a few fresh ingredients with canned ones, or local Thai vegetables with more familiar Western ones, but luckily you can now buy a good selection of cultivated Asian vegetables such as bok choy and napa cabbage. So, with a few careful choices, it's easy to produce some imaginative vegetable dishes with distinctly Thai flavors.

A Thai salad can make a stunning centerpiece for any dinner table. Thai cooks usually add strips of finely chopped cooked meat, fish, or shellfish to their salads, or for vegetarian dishes, mushrooms or tofu are used.

Dressings are typically piquant and spicy, with the usual skillful balance of bitter, salt, sour, hot, and sweet tastes. To finish, a sprinkling of crushed peanuts or dried chiles, chopped cilantro or mint, slices of pickled garlic, and a final flourish of chile flowers or scallion tassels add color.

crisp pickled vegetables

serves 6–8

20 minutes

10 minutes

1/2 small cauliflower
1/2 cucumber
2 carrots
7 oz/200 g green beans
1/2 small Chinese cabbage
generous 2 cups rice vinegar or
    white wine vinegar
1 tbsp superfine sugar

1 tsp salt
3 garlic cloves
3 shallots
3 fresh red Thai chiles, seeded
5 tbsp peanut oil

These crisp, delicately preserved vegetables are usually served as an accompaniment to cooked meat or fish dishes. Thai cooks love to cut vegetables decoratively, and would typically cut the carrots into small flower shapes, but if you're short of time, thin slices look just fine.

cook's tip

To make simple carrot flowers, peel the carrot thinly as usual, then use a canelle knife or small sharp knife to cut narrow "channels" down the length of it at regular intervals. Slice the carrot as usual and the slices will resemble flowers.

Trim the cauliflower. Peel and seed the cucumber. Peel the carrots. Trim the beans. Trim the cabbage, then cut all the vegetables into bite-size pieces. If you have time, cut the carrots into flower shapes (see Cook's Tip).

Place the rice vinegar, sugar, and salt in a large, heavy-bottom pan and bring almost to a boil. Add the vegetables, lower the heat, and let simmer for 3–4 minutes, until they are just tender, but still crisp inside. Remove the pan from the heat and let the vegetables and vinegar cool.

Place the garlic, shallots, and chiles in a mortar and, using a pestle, grind to a smooth paste.

Heat the oil in a skillet. Add the spice paste and stir-fry gently for 1–2 minutes. Add the vegetables with the vinegar and cook for an additional 2 minutes to reduce the liquid slightly. Remove the skillet from the heat and let cool.

Serve the pickles cold, or pack into jars and store in the refrigerator for up to 2 weeks.

chile & coconut sambal

serves 6-8

10 minutes

1 small coconut
1 slice fresh pineapple, finely diced
1 small onion, finely chopped
2 small fresh green chiles, seeded and chopped
2-inch/5-cm piece lemon grass, chopped
½ tsp salt

1 tsp shrimp paste
1 tbsp lime juice
2 tbsp chopped fresh cilantro
fresh cilantro sprigs, to garnish

A sweet-and-sour sambal that goes well with broiled or barbecued fish. It can also be stirred into rice or noodles or even curry dishes as extra flavoring. Adjust the amount of chile to your own taste.

variation

To make a quicker version of this sambal, stir 1 teaspoon Thai green curry paste into freshly grated coconut and add finely diced pineapple and lime juice to taste.

Puncture 2 of the coconut eyes with a screwdriver and pour the milk out from the shell. Crack the coconut shell, prise away the flesh, and coarsely grate it into a bowl.

Mix the coconut with the pineapple, onion, chiles, and lemon grass.

Blend the salt, shrimp paste, and lime juice together in a separate bowl, then stir into the sambal.

Stir in the cilantro. Spoon into a small serving dish and garnish with fresh cilantro sprigs.

mixed vegetables in peanut sauce

serves 4

10 minutes

8–10 minutes

2 carrots
1 small cauliflower, trimmed
2 small heads green bok choy
5½ oz/150 g green beans
2 tbsp vegetable oil
1 garlic clove, finely chopped
6 scallions, sliced
1 tsp chili paste

2 tbsp soy sauce
2 tbsp rice wine or dry sherry
4 tbsp smooth peanut butter
3 tbsp coconut milk

to garnish

1 whole fresh red chile
scallion curls

This colorful mix of vegetables in a rich, spicy peanut sauce can be served either as a side dish or as a vegetarian main course.

cook's tip

It's important to cut the vegetables thinly into even-size pieces so they cook quickly and evenly. Prepare all the vegetables before you start to cook.

Cut the carrots diagonally into thin slices. Cut the cauliflower into small florets, then slice the stalk thinly. Thickly slice the bok choy. Cut the beans into 1¼-inch/3-cm lengths.

Heat the oil in a large skillet or preheated wok. Add the garlic and scallions and stir-fry for 1 minute. Stir in the chili paste and cook for a few seconds.

Add the carrots and cauliflower and stir-fry for 2–3 minutes.

Add the bok choy and beans and stir-fry for an additional 2 minutes. Stir in the soy sauce and rice wine.

Mix the peanut butter with the coconut milk and stir into the skillet, then cook, stirring, for an additional 1 minute. Transfer to a serving dish and garnish with a red chile and scallion curls. Serve hot.

thai **red bean** curry

serves 4

8 minutes

10 minutes

14 oz/400 g green beans
1 garlic clove, finely sliced
1 fresh red Thai chile, seeded
  and chopped
½ tsp paprika
1 piece lemon grass stalk, finely
  chopped

2 tsp Thai fish sauce
½ cup coconut milk
1 tbsp corn oil
2 scallions, sliced

*The "red" in the title refers not to
the beans, but to the sauce, which
has a warm, rusty red color.
This is a good way to serve fresh
beans, and to lift the flavor of
frozen beans too.*

variation

*Young string beans can be used
instead of green beans. Remove any
strings from the beans, then cut at
a diagonal angle in short lengths.
Cook as in the recipe until tender.*

Cut the beans into 2-inch/5-cm pieces and cook in boiling water for
2 minutes. Drain well.

Place the garlic, chile, paprika, lemon grass, fish sauce, and coconut milk in a
blender and process to a smooth paste.

Heat the oil in a skillet or preheated wok. Add the scallions and stir-fry
over high heat for 1 minute. Add the paste and bring the mixture to a boil.

Let simmer for 3–4 minutes to reduce the liquid by about half. Add the
beans and let simmer for an additional 1–2 minutes, until tender. Transfer
to a serving dish and serve hot.

stir-fried ginger mushrooms

serves 4

10 minutes

8 minutes

2 tbsp vegetable oil
3 garlic cloves, crushed
1 tbsp Thai red curry paste
½ tsp ground turmeric
14½ oz/425 g canned Chinese straw
   mushrooms, drained and halved
¾-inch/2-cm piece fresh gingerroot,
   finely shredded
generous ⅓ cup coconut milk
1½ oz/40 g dried Chinese black
   mushrooms, soaked, drained,
   and sliced

1 tbsp lemon juice
1 tbsp light soy sauce
2 tsp sugar
½ tsp salt
8 cherry tomatoes, halved
7 oz/200 g firm tofu, diced
   (drained weight)
fresh cilantro leaves, for sprinkling
freshly cooked fragrant rice, to serve
scallion curls, to garnish

*This quick vegetarian stir-fry is
actually more like a rich curry,
with lots of warm spice and garlic,
balanced with creamy coconut milk.*

variation

*You can vary the mushrooms
depending on your own taste—try
a mixture of oyster and shiitake for
a change—or even just ordinary
cultivated white mushrooms are
delicious cooked in this way.*

Heat the oil in a preheated wok or large skillet. Add the garlic and sauté for 1 minute, stirring. Stir in the curry paste and turmeric and cook for an additional 30 seconds.

Stir in the straw mushrooms and ginger and stir-fry for 2 minutes. Stir in the coconut milk and bring to a boil.

Stir in the Chinese dried black mushrooms, lemon juice, soy sauce, sugar, and salt and heat thoroughly. Add the tomatoes and tofu and toss gently to heat through.

Sprinkle the cilantro over the mixture and serve hot with freshly cooked fragrant rice garnished with scallion curls.

thai-spiced mushrooms

serves 4

10 minutes

10 minutes

8 large flat mushrooms
3 tbsp corn oil
2 tbsp light soy sauce
1 garlic clove, crushed
¾-inch/2-cm piece fresh galangal or
   gingerroot, grated
1 tbsp Thai green curry paste
8 baby corn, sliced
3 scallions, chopped

generous ¾ cup bean sprouts
3½ oz/100 g firm tofu, diced
   (drained weight)
2 tsp sesame seeds, toasted

to serve

chopped cucumber
sliced red bell pepper

*An unusual dish that makes a good
vegetarian main course.
Serve the mushrooms with a
colorful fresh salad.*

cook's tip

*Galangal or ginger can be frozen
for several weeks, either peeled and
finely chopped ready to add to
dishes, or in whole pieces. Thaw the
piece or grate finely from frozen.*

Preheat the broiler to high. Remove the stalks from the mushrooms and set aside. Place the caps on a baking sheet. Mix 2 tablespoons of the oil with 1 tablespoon of the light soy sauce and brush over the mushrooms.

Cook the mushroom caps under the hot broiler until golden and tender, turning them over once.

Meanwhile, chop the mushroom stalks finely. Heat the remaining oil in a large skillet or preheated wok. Add the stalks, garlic and galangal and stir-fry for 1 minute.

Stir in the curry paste, baby corn, and scallions and stir-fry for 1 minute. Add the bean sprouts and stir for an additional 1 minute.

Add the tofu and remaining soy sauce, then toss lightly to heat. Spoon the mixture into the mushroom caps.

Sprinkle with sesame seeds and serve with chopped cucumber and sliced red bell pepper.

asian vegetables with yellow bean sauce

serves 4

2 minutes

8 minutes

1 eggplant
salt
2 tbsp vegetable oil
3 garlic cloves, crushed
4 scallions, chopped
1 small red bell pepper, seeded and
   thinly sliced
4 baby corn, halved
   lengthwise
3 oz/85 g snow peas
7 oz/200 g green bok choy, coarsely
   shredded

14$\frac{1}{2}$ oz/425 g canned Chinese straw
   mushrooms, drained
generous $\frac{3}{4}$ cup bean sprouts
2 tbsp rice wine or dry sherry
2 tbsp yellow bean sauce
2 tbsp dark soy sauce
1 tsp chili sauce
1 tsp sugar
$\frac{1}{2}$ cup chicken or vegetable stock
1 tsp cornstarch
2 tsp water

Serve this colorful mixture of vegetables with a pile of golden, crispy noodles as a vegetarian main course, or on its own to accompany meat dishes.

Cut the eggplant into 2 inch/5 cm long thin sticks. Place in a strainer, sprinkle with salt, and let stand for 30 minutes. Rinse in cold water and dry with paper towels.

Heat the oil in a skillet or preheated wok. Add the garlic, scallions, and bell pepper and stir-fry over high heat for 1 minute. Stir in the eggplant pieces and stir-fry for an additional 1 minute, or until softened.

Stir in the corn and snow peas and stir-fry for 1 minute. Add the bok choy, mushrooms, and bean sprouts and stir-fry for 30 seconds.

Mix the rice wine, yellow bean sauce, soy sauce, chili sauce, and sugar together in a bowl, then add to the skillet with the stock. Bring to a boil, stirring constantly.

Slowly blend the cornstarch with the water to form a smooth paste, then stir quickly into the skillet and cook for an additional 1 minute. Serve at once.

potatoes in
creamed coconut

serves 4

10 minutes

15 minutes

1 lb 5 oz/600 g potatoes	1 1/2 cups vegetable or
1 onion, thinly sliced	chicken stock
2 fresh red Thai chiles, finely chopped	fresh cilantro or basil, chopped,
1/2 tsp salt	to garnish
1/2 tsp pepper	
3 oz/85 g creamed coconut	

A colorful way to serve potatoes, which is quick and easy to make. Serve it with spicy meat curries with a salad on the side.

cook's tip

If the potatoes are a thin-skinned, or a new variety, simply wash or scrub to remove any dirt and cook with the skins on. This adds extra nutrients to the finished dish, and cuts down on the preparation time. Baby new potatoes can be cooked whole.

Using a sharp knife, cut the potatoes into 3/4-inch/2-cm chunks.

Place the potatoes in a pan with the onion, chiles, salt, pepper, and creamed coconut. Stir in the stock.

Bring to a boil, stirring constantly, then lower the heat, cover, and let simmer gently, stirring occasionally, until the potatoes are tender.

Adjust the seasoning to taste if necessary, then sprinkle with chopped cilantro or basil. Serve hot.

stir-fried broccoli in oyster sauce

serves 4

 5 minutes

 6–8 minutes

14 oz/400 g broccoli
1 tbsp peanut oil
2 shallots, finely chopped
1 garlic clove, finely chopped
1 tbsp rice wine or dry sherry
5 tbsp oyster sauce
¼ tsp pepper
1 tsp chili oil

Chinese oyster sauce has a sweet-salty flavor, ideal for adding a richly Asian flavor to plain vegetables. Try this recipe with fresh asparagus when it's in season.

cook's tip

To make chili oil, tuck fresh red or green chiles into a jar and top up with olive oil or a light vegetable oil. Cover with a lid and let infuse for at least 3 weeks before using.

Cut the broccoli into small florets. Blanch in a pan of boiling water for 30 seconds, then drain well.

Heat the oil in a large skillet or preheated wok. Add the shallots and garlic and stir-fry for 1–2 minutes, until golden brown.

Stir in the broccoli and stir-fry for 2 minutes. Add the rice wine and oyster sauce and stir for an additional 1 minute.

Stir in the pepper and drizzle with a little chili oil just before serving.

roasted thai-spiced
bell peppers

serves 4

1 hour 15 minutes

5–10 minutes

2 red bell peppers
2 yellow bell peppers
2 green bell peppers
2 fresh red Thai chiles, seeded and
    finely chopped
1 lemon grass stalk, finely shredded
4 tbsp lime juice
2 tbsp jaggery
1 tbsp Thai fish sauce

*A colorful side dish that also makes
a good buffet party salad.
This dish is best made in advance
to give time for the flavors to
blend together.*

cook's tip

*The flavors will mingle best if the
bell peppers are still slightly warm
when you spoon the dressing over.
Prepare the dressing while the bell
peppers are cooking, so it's ready to
pour over when they are cooked.*

Preheat the broiler, barbecue, or oven to 350°F/180°C. Roast the bell peppers under the hot broiler, barbecue over hot coals, or roast in the oven, turning them over occasionally, until the skins are charred. Let cool slightly, then remove the skins. Cut each in half and remove the core and seeds.

Slice the bell peppers thickly and transfer to a large bowl.

Place the chiles, lemon grass, lime juice, sugar, and fish sauce in a screw-top jar and shake well until thoroughly mixed.

Pour the dressing evenly over the bell peppers. Let cool completely, then cover with plastic wrap and let chill in the refrigerator for at least 1 hour before serving. Transfer to a serving dish to serve.

bok choy
with crabmeat

serves 4

5 minutes

8 minutes

2 heads green bok choy, about 9 oz/
250 g total weight
2 tbsp vegetable oil
1 garlic clove, thinly sliced
2 tbsp oyster sauce
3½ oz/100 g cherry tomatoes, halved
6 oz/175 g canned white crabmeat,
drained
salt and pepper

*Bok choy, also called pak choi,
mustard greens, or Chinese chard,
has a delicate, fresh flavor and crisp
texture, which is best retained by
light, quick cooking. This makes it an
ideal choice for stir-frying.*

variation

*For a vegetarian version of this dish,
omit the crabmeat and replace the
oyster sauce with 2 tablespoons
light soy sauce.*

Using a sharp knife, cut the bok choy into 1-inch/2.5-cm thick slices.

Heat the oil in a large skillet or preheated wok. Add the garlic and stir-fry quickly over high heat for 1 minute.

Add the bok choy and stir-fry for 2–3 minutes, until the leaves wilt, but the stalks are still crisp.

Add the oyster sauce and tomatoes and stir-fry for an additional 1 minute.

Add the crabmeat and season well with salt and pepper. Stir to heat thoroughly and break up the crabmeat before serving.

spiced cashew curry

serves 4	
15 minutes, plus 8 hours soaking	
25 minutes	

scant 2 cups unsalted cashews
1 tsp coriander seeds
1 tsp cumin seeds
2 cardamoms, crushed
1 tbsp corn oil
1 onion, finely sliced
1 garlic clove, crushed
1 small fresh green chile, seeded and chopped
1 cinnamon stick

1/2 tsp ground turmeric
4 tbsp coconut cream
1 1/4 cups hot vegetable stock
3 dried kaffir lime leaves, finely shredded
salt and pepper
fresh cilantro leaves, to garnish
freshly cooked jasmine rice, to serve

This unusual vegetarian dish is best served as a side dish with other curries, either vegetable or meat-based, with rice to soak up the wonderfully rich, spiced juices.

cook's tip

All spices give the best flavor when freshly crushed, but if you prefer, you can use ready-ground spices instead of crushing them yourself using a mortar and pestle.

Place the cashews in a bowl, cover with cold water, and let soak overnight. Drain thoroughly. Crush the coriander, cumin seeds, and cardamoms in a mortar and pestle.

Heat the oil in a large skillet. Add the onion and garlic and stir-fry for 2–3 minutes to soften, but not brown. Add the chile, crushed spices, cinnamon stick, and turmeric and stir-fry for an additional 1 minute.

Add the coconut cream and the hot stock to the skillet. Bring to a boil, then add the cashews and lime leaves.

Cover the skillet, lower the heat, and let simmer for 20 minutes. Serve hot with jasmine rice garnished with cilantro leaves.

potato & spinach
yellow curry

serves 4

5 minutes

15 minutes

2 garlic cloves, finely chopped
1 1/4-inch/3-cm piece fresh galangal,
   finely chopped
1 lemon grass stalk, finely chopped
1 tsp coriander seeds
3 tbsp vegetable oil
2 tsp Thai red curry paste
1/2 tsp ground turmeric
scant 1 cup coconut milk

9 oz/250 g potatoes, cut into
   3/4-inch/2-cm cubes
generous 1/3 cup vegetable stock
generous 4 cups young spinach leaves
1 small onion, thinly sliced into rings

*Potatoes are not highly regarded in
Thai cooking, as rice is the
traditional staple.
This dish is a tasty exception, and
with its luxuriously creamy, golden
coconut sauce, it makes a superb
side dish for any meal.*

cook's tip

*Choose a firm, waxy potato for this
dish, one that will keep its shape
during cooking in preference to a
mealy variety, which will break up
easily once cooked.*

Place the garlic, galangal, lemon grass, and coriander seeds in a mortar and, using a pestle, pound to a smooth paste.

Heat 2 tablespoons of the oil in a skillet or preheated wok. Stir in the garlic paste mixture and stir-fry for 30 seconds. Stir in the curry paste and turmeric, then add the coconut milk and bring to a boil.

Add the potatoes and stock. Return to a boil, then lower the heat and let simmer, uncovered, for 10–12 minutes, or until the potatoes are almost tender.

Stir in the spinach and let simmer until the leaves are wilted.

Meanwhile, heat the remaining oil in a separate skillet. Add the onion and cook until crisp and golden brown.

Place the cooked onions on top of the curry just before serving.

sweet potato cakes

with soy-tomato sauce

serves 4

15 minutes

15 minutes

2 sweet potatoes, I lb 2 oz/500 g
   total weight
2 garlic cloves, crushed
I small fresh green chile, chopped
2 fresh cilantro sprigs, chopped
I tbsp dark soy sauce
all-purpose flour, for dusting
vegetable oil, for cooking
sesame seeds, for sprinkling
fresh cilantro sprigs, to garnish

soy-tomato sauce

2 tsp vegetable oil
I garlic clove, finely chopped
¾-inch/2-cm piece fresh gingerroot,
   finely chopped
3 tomatoes, peeled and chopped
2 tbsp dark soy sauce
I tbsp lime juice
2 tbsp chopped fresh cilantro

Enticing little tasty mouthfuls of sweet potato, served hot and sizzling from the skillet with a delicious fresh tomato sauce.

To make the soy-tomato sauce, heat the oil in a preheated wok. Add the garlic and ginger and stir-fry for 1 minute. Add the tomatoes and stir-fry for an additional 2 minutes. Remove the wok from the heat and stir in the soy sauce, lime, and cilantro. Keep warm.

Peel the sweet potatoes and grate finely (you can do this quickly in a food processor). Place the garlic, chile, and cilantro in a mortar and, using a pestle, crush to a smooth paste. Stir in the soy sauce and mix with the sweet potatoes.

Spread the flour out on a plate. Divide the mixture into 12 equal portions, then dip into the flour and pat into a flat round patty shape.

Heat a shallow layer of oil in a wide skillet. Cook the sweet potato patties over high heat until golden, turning once.

Drain on paper towels and sprinkle with sesame seeds. Transfer to a large serving plate, garnish with cilantro sprigs, and serve hot with the soy-tomato sauce.

thai-style
corn fritters

serves 4

15 minutes

30 minutes

3/8 cup all-purpose flour
1 large egg
2 tsp Thai green curry paste
5 tbsp coconut milk
14 oz/400 g canned or frozen
    corn kernels
4 scallions
1 tbsp chopped fresh cilantro

1 tbsp chopped fresh basil
salt and pepper
vegetable oil, for pan-frying
lime wedges, to garnish
chili relish, to serve

These quick, little fritters can be served as a side dish or a first course, with a spoonful of spicy chili relish and a squeeze of lime juice.

cook's tip

If you prefer to use fresh corn, strip the kernels from the cobs with a sharp knife, then cook in boiling water for 4–5 minutes until just tender. Drain well before using in the recipe.

Place the flour, egg, curry paste, coconut milk, and about half the corn kernels in a food processor and process to a smooth, thick batter.

Finely chop the scallions and stir into the batter with the remaining corn, chopped cilantro, and basil. Season well with salt and pepper.

Heat a small amount of oil in a wide, heavy-based skillet. Drop in table-spoonfuls of the batter and cook for 2–3 minutes, until golden brown.

Turn them over and cook for an additional 2–3 minutes, until golden. Cook in batches, making 12–16 fritters, keeping the cooked fritters hot while you cook the remaining batter.

Transfer the fritters to a serving plate, garnish with lime wedges, and serve with a chili relish.

spicy vegetable fritters with sweet chili dip

serves 4–6

15 minutes

10 minutes

generous 1 cup all-purpose flour
1 tsp ground coriander
1 tsp ground cumin
1 tsp ground turmeric
1 tsp salt
½ tsp pepper
2 garlic cloves, finely chopped
1¼-inch/3-cm piece fresh gingerroot, chopped
2 small fresh green chiles, finely chopped
1 tbsp chopped fresh cilantro
about 1 cup water
1 onion, chopped

1 potato, coarsely grated
3 oz/85 g canned corn kernels
1 small eggplant, diced
4½ oz/125 g Chinese kale, cut into short lengths
coconut oil, for deep-frying

sweet chili dip

2 fresh red Thai chiles, finely chopped
4 tbsp superfine sugar
4 tbsp rice vinegar or white wine vinegar
1 tbsp light soy sauce

These spicy fritters show a clear Indian influence, as they are very similar to pakoras, which are spicy Indian vegetable fritters. They can be served as a first course or as a side dish. The sweet chili dip is a perfect partner.

Make the dip by mixing all the ingredients together thoroughly until the sugar is dissolved. Cover and set aside until required.

For the fritters, place the flour in a bowl and stir in the coriander, cumin, turmeric, salt, and pepper. Add the garlic, ginger, chiles, and cilantro with just enough cold water to form a thick batter.

Add the onion, potato, corn, eggplant, and kale to the batter and stir well to distribute the ingredients evenly.

Heat the oil in a deep skillet or wok to 375°F/190°C, or until a cube of bread browns in 30 seconds. Drop tablespoons of the batter into the hot oil and deep-fry in batches until golden and crisp, turning once.

Drain well on paper towels and serve hot with the sweet chili dip.

eggplant & mushroom
stuffed omelet

serves 1–2

10 minutes

10 minutes

3 tbsp vegetable oil
1 garlic clove, finely chopped
1 small onion, finely chopped
1 small eggplant, diced
½ small green bell pepper, seeded
  and chopped
1 large dried Chinese black
  mushroom, soaked, drained,
  and sliced
1 tomato, diced

1 tbsp light soy sauce
½ tsp sugar
¼ tsp pepper
2 large eggs
dipping sauce, to serve

to garnish

salad greens
tomato wedges
cucumber slices

In Thailand, egg dishes such as this one are eaten as main dishes or snacks, depending on the time of day.

cook's tip

If you heat the skillet thoroughly before adding the oil, and heat the oil before adding the ingredients, you should not have a problem with the ingredients sticking to the skillet.

Heat half the oil in a large skillet. Add the garlic and sauté over high heat for 30 seconds. Add the onion and the eggplant and continue to stir-fry until golden.

Add the green bell pepper and stir-fry for an additional 1 minute to soften. Stir in the mushroom, tomato, soy sauce, sugar, and pepper. Remove from the skillet and keep hot.

Beat the eggs together lightly. Heat the remaining oil in a large, clean skillet, swirling to coat a wide area. Pour in the egg and swirl to set round the skillet.

When the egg is set, spoon the filling into the center. Fold in the sides of the omelet to form a square package.

Slide the omelet carefully onto a warmed dish and garnish with salad greens, tomato wedges, and cucumber slices. Serve with a dipping sauce.

crispy tofu with chile-soy sauce

serves 4

10 minutes

5 minutes

10½ oz/300 g firm tofu
   (drained weight)
2 tbsp vegetable oil
1 garlic clove, sliced
1 carrot, cut into short thin sticks
½ green bell pepper, seeded and cut
   into short thin sticks
1 fresh red Thai chile, seeded and
   finely chopped

2 tbsp soy sauce
1 tbsp lime juice
1 tbsp Thai fish sauce
1 tbsp light brown sugar
pickled garlic slices, to serve
   (optional)

*Tempting golden cubes of cooked
tofu, with colorful fresh carrot and
bell peppers, combine with a warm
ginger sauce to make an unusual
side dish or light lunch dish.*

cook's tip

*Try to buy firm fresh tofu
for this dish. The softer "silken" type
is not firm enough to hold its shape
well during cooking—it is better
for adding to soups.*

Drain the tofu and pat dry with paper towels. Cut the tofu into ¾-inch/
2-cm cubes.

Heat the oil in a preheated wok or large skillet. Add the garlic and stir-fry
for 1 minute. Remove the garlic and add the tofu, then cook quickly until
well browned, turning gently to brown on all sides.

Remove the tofu, drain well, and keep hot. Stir the carrot and bell pepper
into the wok and stir-fry for 1 minute.

Transfer the carrot and bell peppers to a dish and pile the tofu on top.

Mix the chile, soy sauce, lime juice, fish sauce, and sugar together in a bowl,
stirring until the sugar is dissolved.

Spoon the sauce over the tofu and serve topped with pickled garlic slices,
if using. Serve hot.

cucumber salad

serves 4

I hour

–

I cucumber
I tsp salt
I small red onion
I garlic clove, crushed
½ tsp chile paste
2 tsp Thai fish sauce
I tbsp lime juice
I tsp sesame oil

This refreshing spicy salad makes an excellent accompaniment for spicy grilled fish and meat dishes.

cook's tip

Once the salad is made, it can be chilled with the dressing for 1–2 hours, but is best eaten on the day of making.

variation

For a change, peel the cucumber and cut it into small dice, then salt and drain as above. Drain and toss with the onions and dressing as before.

Trim the cucumber and coarsely grate the flesh. Place in a sieve over a large bowl, sprinkle with the salt and leave to stand for 20 minutes. Discard the liquid.

Chop the onion finely, then toss into the cucumber. Spoon into 4 serving bowls. Alternatively, use a large serving dish.

Mix the garlic, chile paste, fish sauce, lime juice and sesame oil together in a bowl then spoon over the salad. Cover and leave to chill before serving.

thai green salad

serves 4–6

12 minutes

–

1 small head cos lettuce
1 bunch of scallions
½ cucumber
4 tbsp coarsely shredded and
   toasted fresh coconut

dressing

4 tbsp lime juice
2 tbsp Thai fish sauce
1 small fresh red Thai chile, finely
   chopped
1 tsp sugar
1 garlic clove, crushed
2 tbsp chopped fresh cilantro
1 tbsp chopped fresh mint

An unusual side salad that is a good accompaniment to any simple Thai main dish, especially broiled meats and fish. Add the dressing just before serving, otherwise the leaves will lose their crispness.

cook's tip

This salad is good for picnics—to pack it easily, pack the leaves into a large plastic container or unbreakable salad bowl, and nestle the jar of dressing in the center. Cover with plastic wrap. Packed this way, the salad stays crisp and if the dressing leaks during transit, there's no mess.

Tear or coarsely shred the lettuce leaves and place in a large salad bowl.

Trim and thinly slice the scallions diagonally, then add them to the salad bowl.

Use a vegetable peeler to shave thin slices along the length of the cucumber and add to the salad bowl.

Place all the ingredients for the dressing in a screw-top jar and shake well to mix thoroughly.

Pour the dressing over the salad and toss well to coat the leaves evenly.

Sprinkle the coconut over the salad and toss in lightly just before serving.

broiled eggplant
& sesame salad

serves 4

1 hour 15 minutes

10 minutes

8 baby eggplants
salt
2 tsp chili oil
1 tbsp soy sauce
1 tbsp Thai fish sauce
1 tbsp corn oil
1 garlic clove, thinly sliced
1 fresh red Thai chile, seeded
    and sliced

1 tsp sesame oil
1 tbsp lime juice
1 tsp light brown sugar
1 tbsp chopped fresh mint
1 tbsp sesame seeds, toasted
fresh mint leaves, to garnish

Eggplants are a popular vegetable in Thailand, as they grow easily throughout the Far East. This dish works well as a first course, but can also be served as an accompaniment to fish or meat dishes.

Cut the eggplants lengthwise into thin slices to within 1 inch/2.5 cm of the stem end. Place in a strainer, sprinkling with salt between the slices, and let stand for 30 minutes. Rinse in cold water and pat dry with paper towels.

Preheat the broiler to medium. Mix the chili oil, soy sauce, and fish sauce together in a bowl, then brush over the eggplants. Cook under the hot broiler, or barbecue over hot coals, for 6–8 minutes, turning them over occasionally and brushing with more chili oil glaze, until golden brown and softened. Arrange on a serving platter.

Heat the corn oil in a large skillet. Add the garlic and chile and sauté for 1–2 minutes, until just starting to brown. Remove the skillet from the heat and add the sesame oil, lime juice, brown sugar, and any remaining chili oil glaze.

Add the chopped mint and spoon the warm dressing over the eggplants.

Let marinate for 20 minutes, then sprinkle with toasted sesame seeds. Serve garnished with mint.

asian lettuce cups

serves 4

15 minutes

–

8 leaves romaine lettuce, or similar
  firm lettuce leaves
2 carrots
2 celery stalks
3 1/2 oz/100 g baby corn
2 scallions
scant 2/3 cup bean sprouts
2 tbsp roasted peanuts, chopped

dressing

2 tbsp smooth peanut butter
3 tbsp lime juice
3 tbsp coconut milk
2 tsp Thai fish sauce
1 tsp superfine sugar
1 tsp grated fresh gingerroot
1/4 tsp Thai red curry paste

A crisp salad with a rich and warmly spiced coconut and peanut dressing, served in pretty lettuce cups.

cook's tip

Choose leaves with a deep cup shape to hold the salad neatly. If you prefer, napa cabbage may be used in place of the romaine lettuce. To remove the leaves from the whole head without tearing them, cut a thick slice from the base end so the leaves are not attached by their stems, then gently ease away the leafy parts.

Wash and trim the lettuce leaves, leaving them whole. Arrange on a serving plate or on individual plates.

Trim the carrots and celery and cut into fine thin sticks. Trim the corn and onions and slice both diagonally.

Toss all the prepared vegetables together with the bean sprouts. Divide the salad mixture evenly between the individual lettuce cups.

To make the dressing, place all the ingredients in a screw-top jar and shake well until thoroughly mixed.

Spoon the dressing evenly over the salad cups and sprinkle with chopped peanuts. Serve at once.

thai-style carrot & mango salad

serves 4

10 minutes

–

4 carrots
1 small, ripe mango
7 oz/200 g firm tofu (drained weight)
1 tbsp snipped fresh chives

dressing

2 tbsp orange juice
1 tbsp lime juice
1 tsp honey
½ tsp orange flower water
1 tsp sesame oil
1 tsp sesame seeds, toasted

A wonderfully refreshing, simple salad to serve as a side dish with hot and spicy meat or fish dishes. It can be prepared 1–2 hours in advance of serving, and chilled in the refrigerator until needed.

cook's tip

A food processor will grate the carrots in seconds, and is especially useful for time-saving if you're catering for a crowd.

Coarsely grate the carrots. Peel, seed, and thinly slice the mango.

Cut the tofu into ½-inch/1-cm dice-shaped pieces and toss together with the carrots and mango in a wide salad bowl.

For the dressing, place all the ingredients in a screw-top jar and shake well until thoroughly mixed.

Pour the dressing over the salad and toss well to coat the salad evenly.

Just before serving, toss the salad lightly and sprinkle with snipped chives. Serve at once.

bamboo shoot salad

serves 4

15 minutes

8–10 minutes

2 shallots
2 garlic cloves
2 tbsp Thai fish sauce
3 tbsp lime juice
$\frac{1}{2}$ tsp dried red pepper flakes
1 tsp granulated sugar
1 tbsp round-grain rice
2 tsp sesame seeds

12 oz/350 g canned bamboo shoots, drained
2 scallions, chopped
napa cabbage or lettuce, shredded, to serve
fresh mint leaves, to garnish

In Thailand, fresh bamboo would always be used for this salad, but canned bamboo shoots make a very good alternative. This dish is usually served to accompany roast pork.

Preheat the broiler to medium. Place the whole shallots and garlic under the hot broiler and cook until charred on the outside and tender inside. Let cool slightly, then remove the skins and discard. Place the flesh in a mortar and using a pestle crush to a smooth paste.

Mix the shallot and garlic paste with the fish sauce, lime juice, red pepper flakes, and sugar in a small bowl.

Place the rice and sesame seeds in a heavy-bottom skillet and cook to a rich golden brown color, shaking the skillet to brown evenly. Remove the skillet from the heat and let cool slightly. Crush the toasted rice and sesame seeds lightly using a mortar and pestle.

Use a sharp knife to shred the bamboo shoots into fine thin sticks and place in a bowl. Stir in the shallot and garlic dressing, tossing well to coat the mixture evenly. Stir in the toasted rice and sesame seeds, then the scallions.

Pile the salad onto a serving dish and surround with shredded napa cabbage. Garnish with mint leaves and serve.

hot & sour beef salad

serves 4

40 minutes

8 minutes

1 tsp black peppercorns
1 tsp coriander seeds
1 dried red bird chile
¼ tsp Chinese five-spice powder
9 oz/250 g beef fillet
1 tbsp dark soy sauce
6 scallions
1 carrot
¼ cucumber
8 radishes
1 red onion
¼ head napa cabbage

2 tbsp peanut oil
1 garlic clove, crushed
1 tsp finely chopped lemon grass
1 tbsp chopped fresh mint
1 tbsp chopped fresh cilantro

dressing

3 tbsp lime juice
1 tbsp light soy sauce
2 tsp light brown sugar
1 tsp sesame oil

Thais are primarily fish-eaters, so beef usually only appears on the menu for feast days. But, as in this dish, a little can go a long way and Thais expertly extend it with exotic mixes of herbs, spices, and colorful vegetables.

Crush the peppercorns, coriander seeds, and chile using a mortar and pestle, then mix with the five-spice powder and sprinkle on a plate. Brush the beef all over with soy sauce, then roll it in the spices to coat evenly.

Cut the scallions into 2½-inch/6-cm lengths, then shred them finely lengthwise. Place in iced water and let stand until curled. Drain well.

Cut the carrot into very thin diagonal slices. Halve the cucumber and scoop out the seeds, then slice thinly. Cut the radishes into flower shapes.

Slice the onion thinly, cutting each slice from top to root. Coarsely shred the napa cabbage. Toss all the vegetables, except the scallion curls, together in a large salad bowl.

Heat the oil in a large, heavy-bottom skillet. Add the garlic and lemon grass and cook until just turning golden brown. Add the steak and press down with a spatula to ensure it browns evenly. Cook for 3–4 minutes, turning it over once, depending on the thickness. Remove the skillet from the heat.

Slice the steak thinly and toss into the salad with the mint and cilantro. Mix the dressing ingredients together in a bowl and stir into the skillet, then spoon over the salad. Garnish with the scallion curls and serve.

desserts & drinks

The normal conclusion to a Thai meal is a basket of fruit, often including mangoes, jackfruit, guavas, litchis, and rambutans. Desserts and candies are mostly made at home for between-meal treats, or made by experts and reserved for special occasions, as their preparation can be time-consuming and often requires skillful blending and shaping.

Even the simplest fruits are prepared in chilled sugar syrups, delicately scented with jasmine or rose, and served with little mouthfuls of sticky rice. Some are gently poached in creamy coconut milk and sweetened or caramelized with jaggery. The banana makes frequent appearances, as bananas grow everywhere, even in gardens.

The ubiquitous coconut plays a large part in sweet recipes, as coconut milk or cream in sweet custards, as delicately scented jellied candies, or shredded for decoration. Rice, usually of the sticky variety, and tapioca are both vital ingredients in many sweets and cakes, often molded or subtly colored, soaked in scented syrups or scented with burning incense.

Many Thai drinks are colorful and exotic in flavor. They use the abundance of fruits and coconut milk in long, refreshing drinks, sweetened with jaggery and often with a dash of whiskey or other spirit.

mangoes in
lemon grass syrup

serves 4

1 hour

5 minutes

2 large, ripe mangoes
1 lime
1 lemon grass stalk, chopped
3 tbsp superfine sugar

A simple, fresh-tasting fruit dessert to round off a rich meal perfectly. Serve the mango lightly chilled.

cook's tip

To serve this dessert on a hot day, particularly if it is to stand for a while, place the dish on a bed of crushed ice to keep the fruit and syrup chilled.

Halve the mangoes, remove the seeds, and peel off the skins.

Slice the flesh into long, thin slices and carefully arrange them in a wide serving dish.

Remove a few shreds of the rind from the lime for decoration, then cut the lime in half and squeeze out the juice.

Place the lime juice in a small pan with the lemon grass and sugar. Heat gently without boiling until the sugar is completely dissolved. Remove the pan from the heat and let cool completely.

Strain the cooled syrup into a small pitcher and pour evenly over the mango slices.

Sprinkle with the lime rind strips, cover, and let chill in the refrigerator before serving. Serve chilled.

exotic fruit salad

serves 6

15–20 minutes

–

1 tsp jasmine tea
1 tsp grated fresh gingerroot
1 strip lime rind
1/2 cup boiling water
2 tbsp superfine sugar
1 papaya
1 mango
1/2 small pineapple
1 carambola
2 passion fruit

This colorful, exotic salad is infused with the delicate flavors of jasmine tea and ginger. Ideally, it should be made and chilled for 1 hour before serving to allow the flavors to develop.

cook's tip

Carambola have little flavor when unripe and green, but once ripened and yellow they become delicately sweet and fragrant. Usually by this stage, the tips of the ridges have become brown, so you will need to remove these before slicing. The easiest and quickest method of doing this is to run a vegetable peeler along each ridge.

Place the tea, ginger, and lime rind in a heatproof pitcher and pour over the boiling water. Let infuse for 5 minutes, then strain the liquid.

Add the sugar to the liquid and stir well to dissolve. Let the syrup stand until it is completely cold.

Halve, seed, and peel the papaya. Halve the mango, remove the seed, and peel. Peel and remove the core from the pineapple. Cut the fruits into bite-size pieces.

Slice the carambola crosswise. Place all the prepared fruits in a wide serving bowl and pour over the cooled syrup. Cover with plastic wrap and let chill in the refrigerator for 1 hour.

Cut the passion fruit in half, scoop out the flesh, and mix with the lime juice. Spoon over the salad and serve.

rose ice

serves 4

3 hours

10 minutes

1¾ cups water
2 tbsp coconut cream
4 tbsp sweetened condensed milk
2 tsp rose water
few drops pink food coloring
   (optional)
pink rose petals, to decorate

A delicately perfumed sweet granita ice, which is coarser than many ice creams. This looks very pretty piled on a glass dish with rose petals sprinkled over.

cook's tip

To prevent the ice thawing too quickly at the table, nestle the base of the serving dish in another dish filled with crushed ice.

Place the water in a small pan and add the coconut cream. Heat the mixture gently without boiling, stirring.

Remove from the heat and let cool. Stir in the condensed milk, rose water, and food coloring, if using.

Pour the mixture into a large, freezerproof container and freeze for 1–1½ hours, or until slushy.

Remove from the freezer and break up the ice crystals with a fork. Return to the freezer and freeze until firm.

Spoon the ice roughly into a pile on a serving dish and sprinkle with rose petals to serve.

mango & lime
sherbet

serves 4

4 hours

4 minutes

scant ½ cup superfine sugar
generous ⅓ cup water
finely grated rind of 3 limes
2 tbsp coconut cream
2 large, ripe mangoes
9 tbsp lime juice
curls of fresh coconut, toasted,
    to decorate

A refreshing sherbet is the perfect way to round off a spicy Thai meal, and mangoes make a deliciously smooth-textured, velvety sherbet.

Place the sugar, water, and lime rind in a small pan and heat gently, stirring constantly, until the sugar dissolves. Boil rapidly for 2 minutes to reduce slightly, then remove from the heat and strain into a bowl or pitcher. Stir in the coconut cream and let cool.

Halve the mangoes, remove the seeds, and peel thinly. Chop the flesh coarsely and place in a food processor with the lime juice. Process to a smooth purée and transfer to a small bowl.

Pour the cooled syrup into the mango purée, mixing evenly. Tip into a freezerproof container and freeze for 1 hour, or until slushy in texture. (Alternatively, use an electric ice-cream maker.)

variation

If you prefer, canned mangoes in syrup can be used to make the sherbet. Omit the sugar and water, and infuse the lime rind in the canned syrup instead.

Remove the container from the freezer and beat with an electric mixer to break up the ice crystals. Refreeze for an additional 1 hour, then remove from the freezer and beat the contents again until smooth.

Cover the container, return to the freezer, and freeze until firm. To serve, remove the sherbet from the freezer and let stand at room temperature for 15 minutes before scooping into individual glass dishes. Sprinkle with toasted coconut and serve.

litchi & ginger
sherbet

serves 4

4 hours

–

1 lb 12 oz/800 g canned litchis
    in syrup
finely grated rind of 1 lime
2 tbsp lime juice
3 tbsp preserved ginger syrup
2 egg whites

to decorate

carambola slices
slivers of preserved ginger

A refreshing palate-cleanser after a rich meal, this sherbet couldn't be easier to make, and can be served either on its own or as a cooling accompaniment to a fruit salad.

cook's tip

It is not recommended that raw eggs are served to very young children, pregnant women, the elderly, or anyone weakened by chronic illness. The egg whites may be left out, but you will need to whisk the sherbet a second time after an additional 1 hour of freezing to obtain a light texture.

Drain the litchis, reserving the syrup. Place the litchis in a blender or food processor with the lime rind, juice, and preserved ginger syrup and process until completely smooth. Transfer to a large bowl.

Mix the purée thoroughly with the reserved litchi syrup, then pour into a large, freezerproof container and freeze for 1–1½ hours, or until slushy in texture. (Alternatively, use an electric ice-cream maker.)

Remove from the freezer and whisk to break up the ice crystals. Whisk the egg whites in a clean, dry bowl until stiff, then quickly and lightly fold into the iced mixture.

Return to the freezer and freeze until firm. Serve the sherbet in scoops, with slices of carambola and ginger to decorate.

pineapple with
cardamom & lime

serves 4

40 minutes

1 minutes

1 pineapple
2 cardamoms
thinly pared lime rind
4 tbsp water
1 tbsp light brown sugar
3 tbsp lime juice

to decorate

fresh mint sprigs
whipped cream

Thai pineapples are sweet and fragrant, and this local fruit appears regularly as a dessert, usually served very simply, but always skillfully sliced and carefully presented.

cook's tip

To remove the "eyes" from pineapple, cut off the peel, then use a small sharp knife to cut a V-shaped channel down the pineapple, cutting diagonally through the lines of brown "eyes" in the flesh, to make spiraling cuts round the fruit.

Cut the top and base from the pineapple, cut away the peel, and remove the "eyes" from the flesh (see Cook's Tip). Cut into quarters and remove the core. Slice the pineapple lengthwise and place in a large serving dish.

Crush the cardamoms in a mortar and pestle and place in a pan with the lime rind and the water. Heat until the mixture is boiling, then let simmer for 30 seconds.

Remove the pan from the heat and add the sugar, then cover and let infuse for 5 minutes.

Stir in the sugar to dissolve, add the lime juice, then strain the syrup over the pineapple. Let chill in the refrigerator for 30 minutes.

When ready to serve, decorate with mint sprigs and whipped cream.

coconut custard squares

serves 4

10 minutes

40 minutes

1 tsp butter, melted
6 eggs
1¾ cups coconut milk
scant 1 cup light brown sugar
pinch of salt
fresh fruit slices, to serve

to decorate

shreds of coconut
strips of lime rind

This easy dessert with an exotic flavor is quite sensuous in texture. It is especially luxurious served with a few slivers of mango or papaya on the side.

cook's tip

Keep an eye on the custard as it bakes, because if it overcooks, the texture will be spoiled. When the custard comes out of the oven, it should be barely set and still slightly wobbly in the center. It will firm up slightly as it cools.

Preheat the oven to 350°F/180°C. Brush the melted butter over the inside of a 7½-inch/19-cm square ovenproof dish, about 1½ inch/4 cm in depth.

Beat the eggs in a large bowl and beat in the coconut milk, sugar, and salt.

Place the bowl over a pan of gently simmering water and stir with a wooden spoon for 15 minutes, or until it starts to thicken. Pour into the prepared dish.

Bake in the preheated oven for 20–25 minutes, until just set. Remove the dish from the oven and let cool completely.

Turn the custard out of the dish and cut into squares. Serve decorated with coconut shreds and strips of lime rind together with slices of fruit.

mung bean
custards

serves 6

40 minutes

50 minutes–1 hour

¾ cup dried mung beans
2 eggs, beaten
¾ cup coconut milk
½ cup superfine sugar
1 tbsp ground rice
1 tsp ground cinnamon, plus extra
   for sprinkling

to decorate
sour cream or whipped cream
finely grated lime rind
sliced carambola
pomegranate seeds

Mung beans give this sweet custard an unusual texture, and it's a real treat served with a generous dollop of sour cream.

cook's tip

To save time, use canned mung beans. Drain the beans thoroughly, mash, and purée and add to the bowl with the eggs and coconut milk.

Preheat the oven to 350°F/180°C. Place the dried mung beans in a pan with enough water to cover. Bring to a boil, then lower the heat and let simmer for 30–40 minutes, until the beans are very tender. Drain well.

Mash the beans, then press through a strainer to form a smooth purée. Place the bean purée, eggs, coconut milk, sugar, ground rice, and cinnamon in a large bowl and beat well until mixed.

Grease and base line 4 x ⅔-cup pudding-shaped molds or ramekins and pour in the mixture. Place on a baking sheet in the preheated oven and bake for 20–25 minutes, or until just set.

Let the custards cool in the molds, then run a knife round the edge to loosen and turn out onto a serving plate. Sprinkle with cinnamon. Decorate with sour cream, lime rind, carambola, and pomegranate seeds.

banana fritters in coconut batter

serves 4

10 minutes

10 minutes

½ cup all-purpose flour
2 tbsp rice flour
1 tbsp superfine sugar
1 egg, separated
⅔ cup coconut milk
4 large bananas
corn oil, for deep-frying

to decorate

1 tsp confectioners' sugar
1 tsp ground cinnamon
lime wedges

This irresistible, classic dessert is best served with a squeeze of lime juice, and topped with a generous spoonful of rich vanilla ice cream.

cook's tip

If you can buy the baby finger bananas that are popular in this dish in the East, leave them whole for coating and deep-frying.

Sift the all-purpose flour, rice flour, and sugar into a bowl and make a well in the center. Add the egg yolk and coconut milk.

Beat the mixture until a smooth, thick batter forms. Whisk the egg white in a clean, dry bowl until stiff soft peaks form. Fold it into the batter lightly and evenly.

Heat a 2½-inch/6-cm depth of oil in a large skillet to 350°F/180°C, or until a cube of bread browns in 30 seconds. Cut the bananas in half cross-wise, then dip them quickly into the batter to coat them.

Drop the bananas carefully into the hot oil and deep-fry in batches for 2–3 minutes, until golden brown, turning once.

Drain on paper towels. Sprinkle with confectioners' sugar and cinnamon and serve at once with lime wedges.

bananas in
coconut milk

serves 4

10 minutes

3–5 minutes

4 large bananas
1 ½ cups coconut milk
2 tbsp superfine sugar
pinch of salt
1 tsp orange flower water
1 tbsp shredded fresh mint
2 tbsp cooked mung beans
fresh mint sprigs, to decorate

An unusual dessert which is equally good served hot or cold. The Thais like to combine fruits and vegetables, so it's not unusual to find mung beans or corn mixed with bananas or other fruits.

variation

If you prefer, the mung beans could be replaced with flaked, toasted almonds, or hazelnuts.

Peel the bananas and cut them into short chunks. Place in a large pan with the coconut milk, superfine sugar, and salt.

Heat gently until boiling and let simmer for 1 minute. Remove the pan from the heat.

Sprinkle the orange flower water over the banana mixture, stir in the mint, and spoon into a serving dish.

Place the mung beans in a heavy-bottom skillet and cook over high heat until turning crisp and golden, shaking the skillet occasionally. Let the beans cool slightly, then crush lightly using a mortar and pestle.

Sprinkle the toasted beans over the bananas and serve warm or cold, decorated with mint sprigs.

caramel apple wedges
with sesame seeds

serves 4

15 minutes

15 minutes

scant 1 cup rice flour
1 egg
½ cup cold water
4 crisp eating apples
2½ tbsp sesame seeds
1¼ cups superfine sugar
2 tbsp vegetable oil, plus extra for
   deep-frying
iced water
fresh basil sprigs, to decorate

A Thai version of a Chinese dessert, these sweet caramel-coated pieces of fruit take practice to perfect, but the trick is to get the timing right. Bananas can also be cooked in this way.

cook's tip

Take care not to overheat the sugar syrup, otherwise it will become difficult to handle and burn. If it starts to set before you have finished dipping the apple pieces, warm it slightly until it becomes liquid again.

Place the flour, egg, and water in a large bowl and whisk well until a smooth, thick batter forms.

Core the apples and cut each into 8 wedges. Drop into the batter and stir in the sesame seeds.

Place the sugar and 2 tablespoons of oil in a heavy-bottom skillet and heat, stirring, until the sugar dissolves. Continue until the syrup starts to turn golden. Remove the skillet from the heat but keep warm.

Heat the oil for deep-frying in a deep skillet or wok to 350°F/180°C, or until a cube of bread browns in 30 seconds. Lift the apple pieces one by one from the batter, using tongs or chopsticks, and lower into the hot oil and deep-fry for 2–3 minutes, until golden brown and crisp.

Remove with a slotted spoon and dip very quickly into the sugar mixture. Dip the apple wedges briefly into iced water and drain on paper towels. Transfer to a serving plate, decorate with basil, and serve at once.

thai rice pudding

serves 4

10 minutes

1 hour 15 minutes

scant ½ cup short-grain rice
2 tbsp jaggery
1 cardamom, split
1¼ cups coconut milk
⅔ cup water
3 eggs

scant 1 cup coconut cream
1½ tbsp superfine sugar
sweetened coconut flakes,
   to decorate
fresh fruit, to serve

This Thai-style version of rice pudding is mildly spiced and creamy, with a rich custard topping. It's excellent served warm, and even better the next day served cold— in Thailand it's even served for breakfast.

cook's tip

Cardamom is quite a powerful spice, so if you find it too strong it can be left out, or replaced with a little ground cinnamon.

Preheat the oven to 350°F/180°C. Place the rice and jaggery in a pan. Crush the seeds from the cardamom using a mortar and pestle and add to the pan. Stir in the coconut milk and water.

Bring to a boil, stirring to dissolve the sugar. Lower the heat and let simmer, uncovered, stirring occasionally for 20 minutes, until the rice is tender and most of the liquid is absorbed.

Spoon the rice into 4 individual ovenproof dishes and spread evenly. Place the dishes in a wide roasting pan with water to come halfway up the sides.

Beat the eggs, coconut cream, and superfine sugar together in a bowl, then spoon over the rice. Cover with foil and bake in the preheated oven for 45–50 minutes, until the custard sets.

Turn out the puddings and decorate the rice puddings with coconut flakes. Serve warm or cold with fresh fruit.

sticky rice shapes

serves 4

15 minutes,
plus 8 hours soaking

35 minutes

scant 1½ cups glutinous rice
generous 2½ cups granulated sugar
1¼ cups water
few drops of rose water or jasmine
    extract
pink and green food colorings
rose petals or jasmine flowers,
    to decorate

*Glutinous rice is the base
for many Thai desserts, and
these little rice shapes are typical.
They're often prettily colored with
food colorings and soaked
in flower-scented syrups,
and children love them.*

cook's tip

*If you prefer, the rice can be
shaped in small sweet molds or
dariole molds to produce small
castle or turret shapes.*

Place the rice in a bowl and add enough cold water to cover. Let soak for 3 hours or overnight.

Drain the rice and rinse thoroughly in cold water.

Line the top part of a steamer with cheesecloth and tip the rice into it. Place over boiling water, then cover and let steam for 30 minutes. Remove the rice from the steamer and let cool.

Heat the sugar and water gently in a pan until the sugar dissolves. Add a few drops of rose water or jasmine extract. Bring to a boil and boil for 4–5 minutes to reduce to a thin syrup. Remove the pan from the heat.

Divide the rice in half and color one half pale pink, the other half pale green. Form into small balls or shapes using molds (see Cook's Tip).

Using 2 forks, dip the rice shapes into the syrup. Drain off the excess syrup and pile onto a dish. Decorate with rose petals or jasmine flowers.

balinese banana
pancakes

serves 6

1 hour 15 minutes

20 minutes

generous 1 cup all-purpose flour
pinch of salt
4 eggs, beaten
2 large, ripe bananas, mashed
1 1/4 cups coconut milk
vegetable oil, for cooking

to decorate

sliced banana
6 tbsp lime juice
confectioners' sugar
coconut cream

These little stacks of rich banana pancakes, drizzled with fragrant lime juice, are quite irresistible at any time of day!

cook's tip

These pancakes are best eaten hot and freshly cooked, so keep them in a low oven while the others are cooking.

Place the flour, salt, eggs, bananas, and coconut milk in a blender or food processor and process to a smooth batter. Alternatively, sift the flour and salt into a bowl and make a well in the center, then add the remaining ingredients and beat well until smooth.

Let the batter chill in the refrigerator for 1 hour. Remove the batter from the refrigerator and beat briefly again. Heat a small amount of oil in a small skillet until very hot.

Drop tablespoonfuls of batter into the skillet. Cook until the pancakes are golden underneath.

Turn over and cook the other side until golden brown. Cook in batches until all the batter is used up, making 36 pancakes. Remove and let drain on paper towels.

Arrange the pancakes in a stack, layered with sliced bananas, sprinkled with lime juice and confectioners' sugar, and served with coconut cream.

coconut crêpes

serves 4

10 minutes

20 minutes

scant 1 cup rice flour
scant 1/4 cup superfine sugar
pinch of salt
2 eggs
2 1/2 cups coconut milk
4 tbsp dry unsweetened coconut
vegetable oil, for cooking
2 tbsp jaggery, to decorate
fresh mango or banana, to serve

These pretty, lacy thin crêpes are sold by Thai street vendors, often colored a delicate pale pink, or tinted green with the juice from pandanus leaves. Add a tiny drop of food coloring if you like, but they look pretty good just as they are, especially served with fresh fruit.

cook's tip

Rice flour gives the crêpes a light, smooth texture, but if it's not available, use all-purpose flour instead.

Place the rice flour, sugar, and salt in a bowl and add the eggs and coconut milk, whisking until a smooth batter forms. Alternatively, place all the ingredients in a blender or food processor and process to a smooth batter. Beat in half the coconut.

Heat a small amount of oil in a wide, heavy-bottom skillet. Pour in a little batter, swirling the skillet to cover the surface thinly and evenly. Cook until pale golden underneath.

Turn the crêpe and cook quickly to brown lightly on the other side.

Remove the crêpe from the skillet and keep hot while using the remaining batter to make a total of 8 crêpes.

Lightly toast the remaining coconut and set aside. Transfer the crêpes folded or loosely rolled to serving plates, sprinkle with jaggery and the toasted coconut, and serve with slices of mango or banana.

steamed coconut cake
with lime & ginger syrup

serves 8

15 minutes

30 minutes

2 large eggs, separated
pinch of salt
1/2 cup superfine sugar
2 3/4 oz/75 g butter, melted
   and cooled
5 tbsp coconut milk
1 cup self-rising flour
1/2 tsp baking powder

3 tbsp dry unsweetened coconut
4 tbsp preserved ginger syrup
3 tbsp lime juice

to decorate

3 pieces preserved ginger
curls of fresh coconut
finely grated lime rind

This steamed coconut cake is very typical of Thai desserts and sweets, and has a distinctly Chinese influence. Eat it in small squares as it's quite rich and sweet.

Cut a 11-inch/28-cm circle of parchment paper and press into a 7-inch/18-cm steamer basket to line it.

Whisk the egg whites with the salt in a clean, dry bowl until stiff. Gradually whisk in the sugar, 1 tablespoon at a time, whisking hard after each addition until the mixture forms stiff peaks.

Whisk in the yolks, then quickly stir in the butter and coconut milk. Sift the flour and baking powder over the mixture, then fold in lightly and evenly with a large metal spoon. Fold in the coconut.

Spoon the mixture into the lined steamer basket and tuck the spare paper over the top. Place the basket over boiling water, cover, and let steam for 30 minutes.

Transfer the cake to a plate, remove the paper, and let cool slightly. Mix the ginger syrup and lime juice together and spoon over the cake. Cut into squares and decorate with preserved ginger, curls of coconut, and lime rind.

strings of gold

serves 4

20 minutes

25 minutes

7 egg yolks
1 tbsp egg white
generous 2½ cups granulated sugar
scant 1 cup water
handful of fresh scented jasmine
    flowers

to decorate

pomegranate seeds
sliced kiwifruit
sliced apple

These golden egg threads take a little practice, but they're a very traditional Thai dessert, so well worth a try. The little coils of threads are meant to represent the hands placed together in a traditional Thai greeting. The Thais use a special tool to drizzle the egg in fine streams, but you can use a pastry bag.

Press the egg yolks and egg white through a fine strainer. Whisk lightly.

Place the sugar and water in a large pan and heat gently until the sugar dissolves. Add the jasmine flowers, bring to a boil and boil rapidly until a thin syrup forms. Remove the flowers with a slotted spoon.

Bring the syrup to the simmering point. Using a pastry bag with a fine tip quickly drizzle the egg mixture into the syrup in a thin stream to form loose nests or pyramid shapes.

As soon as the threads set, remove the nests carefully and drain well on paper towels. Arrange in a warmed serving dish and decorate with the pomegranate seeds, kiwifruit, and apple. Serve at once.

variation

If you can't get hold of fresh, scented jasmine flowers, add a few drops of rose water or orange flower water to the syrup instead.

melon
& ginger crush

serves 4

5 minutes

–

1 melon, about 1 lb 12 oz/800 g
6 tbsp ginger wine
3 tbsp kaffir lime juice
crushed ice
1 lime

A really refreshing summer drink, this melon crush is quick and simple to make. If you can't buy kaffir limes, ordinary limes are fine.

variation

If you prefer a nonalcoholic version of this drink, simply omit the ginger wine, then top up with ginger ale in the glass. For a change of flavor, use a watermelon when they are in season. Ginger wine is available from specialist wine merchants.

Peel, seed, and coarsely chop the melon. Place the melon in a blender or food processor with the ginger wine and lime juice.

Blend together on high speed until the melon mixture is smooth.

Place plenty of crushed ice in 4 medium straight-sided glasses. Pour the melon and ginger crush over the ice.

Cut the lime into thin slices, cut a slit in 4 of the slices, and slip one onto the side of each glass. Add the remaining slices of lime to each glass, then serve at once.

mango &
coconut smoothie

serves 4

5 minutes

–

2 large, ripe mangoes
1 tbsp confectioners' sugar
scant 2½ cups coconut milk
5 ice cubes
flaked, toasted coconut, to serve

A velvety smooth, delicately scented drink without alcohol. This can be served at any time of day—even for breakfast.

cook's tip

To add a special kick to the drink (though not perhaps for breakfast!), add a generous dash of white rum to the blender with the coconut milk.

variation

If you don't have shredded, toasted coconut, sprinkle with ground ginger, cinnamon, or nutmeg just before serving.

Using a sharp knife, cut the mangoes in half and remove the seed. Peel and coarsely chop the flesh.

Place the chopped mango flesh in a blender or food processor with the confectioners' sugar and process until completely smooth.

Add the coconut milk and ice to the blender and process until frothy.

Pour into 4 tall glasses and sprinkle with flaked, toasted coconut to serve.

lime
& lemon grass cooler

serves 4

5 minutes

—

egg white
3 tbsp superfine sugar, plus extra
    for frosting
2 limes
1 small lemon grass stalk
4 ice cubes
½ cup water
4 lime slices
club soda

*This cooling, nonalcoholic cocktail
looks delightful served in tall
glasses with frosted rims.
If you're after something stronger,
add a shot of gin or vodka
to each glass.*

cook's tip

*It's important not
to blend the limes for
too long—a few seconds
is enough to chop them finely
and extract the juice. If you
overprocess, the drink will
have a bitter flavor.*

To frost the rim of the glasses, pour a little egg white into a saucer. Spread a small amount of superfine sugar out on a plate. Dip the rim of each glass briefly into egg white, then into the superfine sugar.

Cut each lime into 8 pieces and coarsely chop the lemon grass. Place the lime pieces and lemon grass in a blender or food processor with the sugar and ice cubes.

Add the water and process for a few seconds.

Strain the mixture into the frosted glasses. Add a lime slice to each glass and top off with club soda to taste. Serve at once.

thai cocktail sling

serves 1

5 minutes

2 tbsp whiskey
1 tbsp cherry brandy
1 tbsp orange-flavored liqueur
1 tbsp lime juice
1 tsp jaggery
dash of Angostura bitters
2 ice cubes
1/2 cup pineapple juice
1 small pineapple wedge

A Thai-style version of a much more classic cocktail, this is a long drink with a strong kick of whiskey.

cook's tips

If the pineapple juice is quite sweet, as Thai pineapple juice is, you may not need to add sugar. So if you're unsure, taste first.

Scotch whisky is very highly regarded in Thailand, although a powerful whiskey is distilled locally—if you have the stomach for it!

Place the whiskey, cherry brandy, liqueur, lime juice, jaggery, and Angostura bitters in a cocktail shaker. Shake well to mix thoroughly.

Place the ice cubes in a large glass. Pour the cocktail mixture over the ice, then top off with the pineapple juice.

Cut a slit in the pineapple wedge and arrange on the edge of the glass. Serve at once.

tropical fruit punch

serves 6

5 minutes

–

1 small ripe mango
4 tbsp lime juice
1 tsp finely grated fresh gingerroot
1 tbsp light brown sugar
1 1/4 cups orange juice
1 1/4 cups pineapple juice
generous 1/3 cup rum
crushed ice

to decorate

orange slices
lime slices
pineapple slices
carambola slices

This exotic looking cocktail is simplicity itself, and can be varied with different fruit juices. Top with lavish amounts of fruit for a really festive effect.

cook's tip

To extend the drink a little further, and bring out the ginger flavor, top up each glass with a generous dash of ginger ale.

Peel and seed the mango and chop the flesh. Place in a blender or food processor with the lime juice, ginger, and sugar and process until smooth.

Add the orange and pineapple juice, then add the rum and process again for a few seconds until blended.

Divide the crushed ice between 6 glasses and pour the punch over the ice.

Add orange and lime slices, then arrange the pineapple and carambola on the rim of each glass. Serve at once.

Index